P9-DUX-727

THE PRICE OF THEIR BLOOD

PROFILES IN SPIRIT

Jesse Brown
and Daniel Paisner
Foreword by Lois Pope

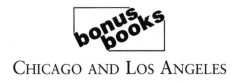

CHICAGO AND LOS ANGELES

© 2003 by The Lois Pope Life Foundation
All rights reserved

Except for appropriate use in critical reviews or works of schol-
arship, the reproduction or use of this work in any form or by
any electronic, mechanical, or other means now known or here-
after invented, including photocopying and recording, and in any
information storage and retrieval system is forbidden without the
written permission of the publisher.

07 06 05 04 03 5 4 3 2 1

Library of Congress Control Number: 2003112767

Bonus Books
875 N. Michigan Ave.
Suite 1416
Chicago, IL 60611

Printed in the United States of America

To all American servicemen
and women

"I cannot omit to mention the obligations this Country is under, to that meritorious Class of veteran Non-commissioned Officers and Privates, who have been discharged for inability . . . nothing but a punctual payment of their annual allowance can rescue them from the most complicated misery, and nothing could be a more melancholly and distressing sight, than to behold those who have shed their blood or lost their limbs in the service of their Country, without a shelter, without a Friend, and without the means of obtaining any of the necessaries or comforts of life, compelled to beg their daily bread from door to door! . . . It was a part of their hire, I may be allowed to say, it was the price of their blood and of your Independency, it is therefore more than a common debt, it is a debt of honor, it can never be considered as a pension or gratuity, nor be cancelled untill it is fairly discharged . . . "

—George Washington
from an unpublished circular letter of
farewell to Army leaders
June 8, 1783
Newburgh, New York

CONTENTS

FOREWORD

When Jesse Brown died in 2002, American veterans lost a great advocate—and I lost a treasured friend.

Just over two years ago, I envisioned a book that would honor the millions of unsung heroes of America's armed forces who have become disabled for life while defending our freedom. Jesse, with his trademark humility, suggested that I should lead this project, but I knew that it was Jesse's pen that would leave an indelible mark of gratitude and respect on the courageous stories of the disabled veterans profiled. And so this very special project began.

While I am profoundly saddened by Jesse's passing, he has left us much to celebrate. Jesse was a true American hero who lifted himself to greatness, not in spite of his disability, but perhaps because of it. He rose from adversity and was an inspiration to us all.

Jesse was a United States Marine. Wounded during combat in Vietnam in 1965, he lost the use of his right arm, but Jesse returned home undeterred by his disability and inspired to help his fellow disabled veterans, many of whom had suffered wounds far worse than his. He soon became a dedicated veterans' advocate. When he joined the staff of the Disabled American Veterans, Jesse began the work that would become not only his profession, but his life. In 1993, Jesse's outstanding achievements on behalf of veterans were recognized when President Clinton appointed him as secretary of the Department of Veterans Affairs. Among his many accomplishments, Jesse's greatest source of pride was his effort to make the Department of Veterans Affairs an enterprise that "puts veterans first." Jesse's proud service to our nation and his relentless advocacy on behalf of all veterans earned him the distinction of being known as the Secretary FOR Veterans Affairs.

After leaving the president's cabinet, Jesse continued his life's work by diving headlong into the campaign to build the American Veterans Disabled for Life Memorial, a memorial in Washington, D.C. to commemorate the sacrifice and dedication of all disabled veterans and ensure that they are always remembered.

Jesse understood better than anyone that all Americans owe our disabled veterans a debt of both gratitude and honor. They answered the call when our nation needed them. He also understood that it is both fitting and necessary that we honor the 2.3 million disabled veterans living among us today, as well as those who came before them, with a memorial in the Federal City, where visitors from near and far will learn of the legacy of America's disabled veterans: their sacrifice, their struggle, and, ultimately, their accomplishments in meeting life's most unrelenting challenges.

As usual, Jesse said it best: "Our memorial will be a place of special distinction, a place where Americans can go to simply say thank you to 500 veterans who lost both arms while serving in the military; 17,000 paralyzed veterans whose sense of activity is forever changed; and 12,000 veterans who are totally blind, able to see colors and beauty only in their minds."

Through Jesse's work and the dedication of many others who wish to repay this debt, that memorial is becoming a reality.

Until his death in the summer of 2002, Jesse remained highly engaged in this important initiative, even as Lou Gehrig's disease robbed him of nearly all of his physical abilities.

Through the lifelong friends that he made in his untiring dedication to America's veterans and through his unflagging commitment to *The Price of Their Blood: Profiles in Spirit*, Jesse leaves us a final gift—his message of the conviction that, with hard work, courage, and determination, a disability is no handicap, that goals can be achieved, that life's vicissitudes are no barrier, that dreams have no limits.

The unsung heroes profiled in this book fit this characterization. The pages of this book are filled with ordinary people who have overcome extraordinary hardships. Each and every day, these inspiring individuals live their lives to the beat of the same drum as my dear friend and personal hero, Jesse Brown. And, like Jesse, they are an inspiration to us all.

A great person is said to be one who overcomes adversity. An even greater person inspires others to do the same. Jesse was, for me and for millions of other Americans, that greater person, that inspiration. And though I am writing after his death, true heroes never die. They remain secure in our hearts, in the works they performed, and in the seeds of inspiration that they sowed on their journey through life. Jesse believed in the power of dreams. His works and continuing legacy survive and inspire others to achieve all that they can dream to be and more.

I'm deeply pleased to see my vision for this book come to life. And how I wish Jesse were here to share in yet another of his many accomplishments. It is an honor for me to help celebrate this meaningful book and the precious life and continuing legacy of my dear friend, Jesse Brown.

Lois Pope, founder, the Lois Pope LIFE Foundation
and Leaders in Furthering Education (LIFE)
September, 2003

MISSION STATEMENT

Jesse Brown with President Bill Clinton

For most of my adult life, folks have been telling me to sit down and write a book, and I've always resisted the notion. The suggestion has typically been that with my experiences on the front lines in Vietnam and on the front lines of various advocacy efforts for our veterans at home, I must have a few volumes of stories to tell. I suppose this is true, but it's not me. I suppose it's also true that my experiences and accomplishments on behalf of our servicemen and women offer a kind of blueprint for helping to nourish and sustain American veterans in the future, as has also been suggested, but that's not me either. Leave it to someone else to judge my place in history or to revisit (or second guess!) my positions and initiatives. And leave it to someone else to chronicle my personal experiences in and around Vietnam (if anyone is so inclined) because I've never been one for telling dramatic stories on myself. Once again, it's just not me.

It's an interesting paradox, I'll admit: I've lived a fairly public life for an essentially private man, and yet I could never see forsaking what little privacy was left to me and my family by publishing my memoirs. I'm much more interested in shining a light on some of the wonderfully courageous and inspiring veterans I've befriended as secretary of veterans affairs under President Bill Clinton and throughout my long career at the Disabled American Veterans, which is why when the idea for this book came up, my feelings changed. This, I immediately thought, was more like it. This was more like me.

Ask my mother. Ask my wife. Ask my children. Ask my many friends and colleagues. They'll all tell you the same. At the end of the day, what gets me talking and keeps me going are the heroic men and women who cross my path, the names and faces attached to the statistics and policies that informed my tenure in the president's cabinet and my endlessly fulfilling work at the DAV. The "citizen" soldiers who gave everything for their country, and a little bit more besides. The anonymous veterans whose selfless sacrifice marked their lives going forward. Indeed, for every tragic story of a life unraveled by military battle, there are a dozen tales of individuals who have managed to triumph over the harrowing experiences of war and ruin—and this book is a tribute to those triumphs. It's a collection of motivating, inspiriting profiles of some of America's truly "unsung" heroes—stretching from a World War One veteran believed to be the oldest living combat-wounded serviceman in the United States at the time of this writing, up to a daring Green Beret caught in friendly fire in the unconventional, unrelenting war on terrorism in the Middle East that continues to dominate the world stage.

One of the clinchers for me in deciding to take on this project was that it wasn't about me. It's about my fellow veterans—my fellow *disabled* veterans—for I've always believed that in holding a mirror to the past, we can see where we've been and where we're going. And that's not all: I also believe that those who have put their lives on the line for their country deserve to be treated with dignity and respect, and this has been a hallmark of my advocacy work. This is especially so for our combat-wounded veterans and prisoners of war who return from service with those lives still very much on the line. There are life-threatening injuries to confront and surmount, life-changing disabilities to meet and master, and life-shaping experiences to make peace with and understand. These lives on the line are all over these pages.

The other clincher was that this book promised to call important attention to the shared effort to build a national memorial to disabled American veterans near the U.S. Capitol in Washington, D.C. In all my years of public service, I've learned to never underestimate the power of the media, and it's a learned truth that a well-received book can become a kind of platform for a related issue. That's what I'm hoping for here, that the powerful stories shared in this book will bring compelling focus on the memorial project. It's a joint effort of the DAV, under National Adjutant Arthur H. Wilson, and the LIFE Foundation, headed by my good friend, the philanthropist Lois B. Pope, and, upon completion, the memorial promises to stand as a beacon and a touchstone—a great, unifying emblem of disabled veterans and the citizens for whom they sacrificed so much. The American Veterans Disabled for Life Memorial, funded entirely by private contributions, will honor the millions of veterans of the Armed Forces who became disabled for life while defending America's freedom, and provide a vibrant reminder of war's true human cost. Too, the sight of the memorial will remind legislators and visitors to our nation's capital that disabled veterans throughout American history have paid an enduring price for our freedoms at home and abroad. I can't stress how excited I am to see this noble ideal become a reality, and I set these thoughts to paper convinced that the book you now hold in your hands will lend a resounding exclamation point to the development of the memorial, for it is in the living, breathing testimony of these rebuilt life stories that the struggles of our wounded veterans truly come alive.

All of which brings me to the living, breathing testimony that echoes through these pages—one patriotic life after another, linked by the struggle for a new existence, challenged by one disability or another, and connected by a kind of friendship. Yes, these good people are my good friends, collected and cherished over the years along with countless others, and their stories offer inspiration and hope. Some will make you cry. Some will make you laugh. Most will make you do a little bit of both because I've found—as my friend Bobby Barrera suggests in the uplifting presentation he gives to groups around the country—that a rich sense of humor is almost always a key to overcoming life's obstacles.

The common threads to these personal histories are our shared commitment to the American way of life, our love of God and country, and our unflagging support for each other, in good times and bad. In my unit in Vietnam, we had folks with very different personalities, from very different backgrounds, with very different views, and yet we all worked together. Under fire, you would have never seen all those differences for our shared purpose and sense of mission. When I was wounded, four Marines—of different races—came to my rescue, and as they tended to me and helped to put my mind at ease, I took great comfort in knowing that we were all of a piece. We were different, but underneath we were the same.

So it is with the men and women profiled here. Their accounts have helped to shape my life, as their friendships have given it color and meaning. I trust that they will touch your life as well.

Jesse Brown
May, 2002

ACKNOWLEDGMENTS

This book could not have been completed (or, indeed, undertaken), without the generous support and enthusiasm of the following individuals: Sylvia Brown, Lois Pope, Charlie Thompson, Art Wilson, Dan Klores, Jeff Stern, Mel Berger, Bob Miller, Kelley Thornton, and Bruce Bobbins.

THE PRICE OF
THEIR BLOOD

WAR AND PEACE

Photo by Marcy Holquist

Michael A. Naranjo
U.S. Army, Vietnam War

Sometimes, the measure of a man is taken with a graceful line in a block of stone. So it is with Michael Naranjo, a soft-spoken, gentle spirit whose own line has taken him from Native American tribal land to an ambush in an open rice field in Vietnam that cost him his eyesight and the principle use of his right arm, and back to his native New Mexico, where he seems about as far removed from tension and conflict as a person has any right to be.

A gentle, cherubic man with graying hair like steel wool, a face leathered comfortably by the sun, and a firm grip that belies his peaceful demeanor, Naranjo is an internationally renowned sculptor, whose work has been displayed in public and private collections all around the world. His work reflects the left-behind visions of his of his youth, a view of the world colored by the hope and harmony of nature, and it has been featured in prominent exhibitions and museum spaces celebrating the art of the American West.

Those who don't know Naranjo by name remember him as "the artist who sees with his hands," and it is a fitting description for a man who refuses to let his blindness cloud his vision. Indeed, his work has been his passion and his balm, and it grew out of a tossed-off request of a volunteer at an American army hospital in Japan, where Naranjo was recuperating from the kinds of wounds that might have stilled a lesser spirit. The seeds were already there, but they grew on a whim. He asked for some water-based clay to keep him company in those dark, early days of recovery. Naranjo's mother, Rose, had been an accomplished potter, and Naranjo had had his hands in her clay since he was a boy. The clay struck him as something to do, a way to fill the time. He didn't think things through to where the clay might stand as a kind of bridge to help him cross from darkness into light, but he might have. A few days later, the volunteer returned to Naranjo's side with a mound of clay. She set the clay on the hospital tray table that swung over his bed, and she took his left hand and placed it on the clay. That was about the last thing Naranjo remembered for a while, lost as he became in the clay and where it took him.

"I let it sit there for a time," he recalls more than thirty-five years later, "and eventually I tore off a piece, and without really thinking about it I started to roll the clay around in my fingers. I thought of all the pieces I used to sculpt as a child: deer, bear, birds, buffaloes—all the different animals my brother and I used to see on the reservation. And as I was thinking, I was working the clay with my hands, rolling it up into a ball, smoothing it out, getting used to the feel of it. I didn't really think it through, but it made itself into a little inchworm. I made a little mouth with my thumbnail, found little beads to use for eyes. A crazy little inchworm. And the moment I'd finished, I knew I'd be okay."

The moment before, he'd known no such thing. He had no idea. All he knew, as he lay in his hospital bed, was his new, uncertain reality. All he knew was that he'd lost his sight, and, for the time being, the use of his right hand. To these losses, he added hope and urgency and any abiding sense that all would be right in his world. For a time, army doctors didn't know if he would even survive, he'd been wounded so badly, so thoroughly. But here he was, on the mend, finally, a ray of hope alighting where there had been no hope at all. He had been weighing where he was against where he'd been and, in the balance, couldn't imagine where he might be going—until that inchworm came along.

"I wish I still had it," he says now of that first piece. He made another piece, and another, and he sent for more clay. As he waited for it, he realized he now had something to look forward to. A place to put his energy and ambition. A locus for healing. A way to look back on a world he could no longer see.

Naranjo grew up in New Mexico on the Santa Clara Pueblo, approximately thirty miles north of Santa Fe. He was one of ten children. He spoke Tewa, the language of the reservation, which covered approximately seventy-five square miles. It was a self-contained environment. There was a school that ran to the eighth grade. There was a small clinic and a market. There was a community of people who looked out for each other and for each other's children. Naranjo's father was a

carpenter—he was part of a team of construction workers that helped to build Los Alamos—but he built the
balance of his life as a Baptist minister. His mother, the
potter, was an artist, and she encouraged her children to
develop their own visions, to look beyond themselves
and the reservation and to see the world around them.

It was, to hear Naranjo tell it, an almost heavenly
childhood. "I was extremely close to my brother Tito
when I was growing up," he says. "He was everything to
me: brother, father, friend, mentor. We used to do a lot of
hunting and fishing together, things like that. Tito would
wake me at daybreak, and we'd run along the foot trails
in the valley, three or four miles or so, and then we'd
come home. There was a sign over our bedroom door
that read, 'Thrust against pain because pain is the purifier and the keeper of wisdom,' and we'd come home all
tired from our run and consider the meaning of that. At
the end of the day, we'd run at the other end of the valley,
another three or four miles, this time with the buffaloes.
We'd run wind sprints along a fence that had been set up
there, a half-mile or so at a sprint, against this beautiful
scenery, and the rest of the world was so very far away."

Of course, the rest of the world wasn't so far away
that it wouldn't eventually reach Michael Naranjo. The
war in Vietnam was soon enough on his radar as he began
his public schooling in the small town of Taos, New Mexico, which is cradled in the corner of a large valley in the
shadow of the mountains. It was hopelessly beautiful
country, and Naranjo would have to take in enough of
that beauty to last a lifetime. The protests and upheaval
of the 1960s didn't quite reach that part of the world—"I

even missed the Beatles," he says, "the importance of them"—but news of the war came through loud and clear. When he thought about it at all, he thought about joining the navy; he couldn't picture himself on a battlefield, weapon in hand, steeled for combat—it wasn't his nature. On a ship, he thought, his chances for survival would be far greater; on a ship, he might convince himself that his mission was something other than destruction; on a ship, he might be off to see the world.

"I got as far as the navy recruiting office," he says, "and I sat there with a friend of mine, filling out our applications, and I was about to hand it in and I thought, three years? I couldn't see signing on for such a long tour. It seemed like the longest time, like a lifetime, especially because at that time, it was still unclear if I'd even be called in the draft. So I decided I'd take my chances. I crumpled up that application and threw it in the wastebasket and walked out."

He took his chances to a small college in Texas, and then on to an even smaller college in Las Vegas, New Mexico, but he'd never been much of a student. His brothers and sisters would all go on to get their college degrees—advance degrees, even—but Michael would do the bare minimum to get by. His interests lay elsewhere, outside the confining walls of a classroom. In the back of his mind, he returned to his mother's studio and thought he might some day become a sculptor, although he made no proactive moves in this direction, either. He had the thought, and then he set it aside. He took a construction job. He got married. "The marriage only lasted a short time," he says, "and I don't think I stayed on that job for too long, either. I was a lost child, back then. I didn't have a clear idea what I wanted to do, what I was meant to do."

He still couldn't see himself as a soldier, and his ears pricked up when he heard other young men talk about moving to Canada, but he had no real desire to do that. It wasn't in him to run. When his number was called, he figured he'd take his chances yet again. "When you're young," he reflects, "you're invincible. You're immortal. I thought I'd come back. Perhaps I wouldn't, there was that thought, too, but I had this feeling that I would come back. Underneath that feeling, there was another, that maybe I wouldn't be quite the same, but I felt I'd make it back."

Naranjo was sent to Vietnam in November, 1967, after a stint at Fort Knox, Kentucky, for armored personnel carrier training. He left from California and ended up in Bien Hoa, where he'd been assigned. Naranjo's reflections on those first moments in country are unique. "It was a very strange world," he says, "and I was struck by all these Vietnamese women walking down the road with their black, flowing robes. Some of them wore a kind of mini-dress, and I remember thinking the contrast so very strange, these flowing robes and mini-dresses against the stark backdrop of the countryside. It was all so very beautiful, and from time to time the women would look at me and point and say, 'You same-same.' And I supposed I was. With my features and my dark complexion, I could have been one of them."

When he speaks, Michael Naranjo chooses his words carefully, meticulously, as if carving his thoughts with the same precision he might bring to a block of wood. He speaks, for example, of the difficulties he experienced adjusting from the wide-open spaces of his youth, the boundless, open environment of the reservation, to the rigid, regimented environment of the United States Army in a time of war. He pauses on this contrast for some time before landing softly on this notion: "Your identity is lost," he says. "You find yourself carving out your own freedoms."

He thinks back to his advance infantry training in Louisiana, ducking out of K.P. because he couldn't see the point, because he knew the duty would get done without him, and because someday he would be covering for a friend who ducked out in the same way. There were other dodges, too. "I can still picture it," he says. "I can still see myself in those moments, a skinny kid, marching down towards this area, in the hot Louisiana sun, across these great bleachers they had set up on the base, meandering down this pathway, our drill sergeant up at the head, and at the other end we'd have to sit through this or that drill, or learn this or that tactic. It was so difficult at times to stay awake. We were so tired. It was so hot. So I'd duck out when I could, into the brush, where maybe it was a little cooler, or maybe I could lay back and enjoy the sun for an hour or so. I knew they'd be back in an hour or so, and that they wouldn't miss me. Was I crazy? Perhaps. Down the road, what did I miss by ducking out on these marches? Would I have learned something that might have saved me in that rice field? Perhaps. But that was my nature."

At twenty-three, Naranjo was somewhat older than most of the young men in his platoon, but he doesn't recall feeling any older. They were all just boys, he says, all too young to be sent to do the work of men, too young to understand what it might mean. The differences between them had more to do with battlefield experience than age. "I noticed these differences in basic training," he explains, "and I couldn't understand it at first. The difference between those of us just sitting there, just starting out, and those of us who'd already been overseas and come back. There was a hardness to some of those instructors, the ones who'd been to Vietnam, and once I got there I understood that hardness. It's a shell you need to develop on the battlefield, a protection from the horrors of war. You have to separate yourself from what you're doing, emotionally, to preserve your sanity. If you don't do that, I can't imagine how you get through it, and I noticed that in others before I experienced it for myself. And I accepted it as part of my evolution as a soldier. I wanted to understand it."

Naranjo also wanted to understand what it meant to shoot another man. If it had been up to him, he never would have been in a position to consider the dilemma, but now that he was, he wanted to consider it fully. In this, he stands apart from the majority of American soldiers, who are taught to shoot without thinking. Understanding usually comes somewhat further down the list, but not for Michael Naranjo. In this way, and in others, his tour of duty was like a constant puzzle: he came away thinking if he studied it from every possible angle, he might make the pieces fit. He might make sense of it. He worked to know that hardness he witnessed in his instructors, the hardness he saw in his veteran platoon members, the hardness he knew would overtake him in the nippa palm bushes that dotted the rice fields in and around the countryside. Finally, some weeks into his tour, that hardness found him. He stood nearly face to face with a North Vietnamese soldier. Naranjo was clearing a field for booby traps, walking point for his squad, when all of a sudden a man popped out of the grass out in front of him, not fifty yards away. They were at the edge of a field, a couple of steps from water, and, as far as Naranjo could tell, it was just the two of them.

"It was very hot," he now recalls, "and I stared at this man for what seemed the longest time. And he stared back. In truth, it must have only been a fraction of a second, but it felt a lot longer. And he had this look about him that seemed to say, 'Well, then, here we are.' Like resignation. And I fired, and he went down. It was the strangest thing."

And there was that hardness. Naranjo had been expecting it, searching for it, and there it was. In that one brief moment, that fraction of a second, he might have heard the voices of those Vietnamese women— "You same-same!"—because there wasn't much to separate the two enemies beyond those fifty yards, the colors of their uniforms, and their ideologies.

January 8, 1968. Naranjo's platoon had been bombarded the night before. He was holed up behind a sandbag wall, and, to his ears, the shelling sounded slightly different than the big, big guns he was used to hearing, slightly more ominous. There was a news crew traveling with the 9th Infantry, and Naranjo recalls that this added to the general commotion of the shelling. At this point, two months in country, Naranjo was feeling a kind of immunity, to where he got to thinking that if he was going to be hit in one area of the camp, he would be hit behind the sandbag wall as well. He wasn't reckless, he insists, but at the same time, he wasn't placing much stock in a false sense of protection. So he moved about freely, making ready, doing what he had to do. He moved with his platoon to a waiting chopper, which took them to a nearby rice field. The open field was set in the shape of a T, flanked by high nippa palm bushes, abutting a thick jungle. There was already a squad up ahead of them, crossing the field, when Naranjo's squad set down and fell in behind.

"We all had a sense that something was about to happen," he says. "Everyone was anticipating some battle or gunfire or engagement of some kind, and we crossed that field like we had a job to do. Of course, as soon as we were out in the open, the Vietcong started shooting. We had been led into an ambush."

There was no cover, save for the ground and a dike that ran along the field. Naranjo looked up at the first sound of gunfire, and, from his low position, he could see two soldiers in the squad up ahead as they crumbled to the ground. Two men he knew—dead, certainly, from the way they fell. Naranjo hit the dirt. For a few seconds, the field was silent. Nobody moved. Naranjo waited for a long beat. In the pause between reports, Naranjo sprang to his feet and advanced, charging ahead until the next round sent him back down. "We'd move about ten or fifteen yards at a clip," he guesses. "I knew they'd keep shooting, but we had to cross that field. Eventually, knowing that I couldn't go any further, I rolled over the dyke. Out of the corner of my eye, I could see others hitting the dirt. I saw two men hit, not five yards from me. The platoon sergeant reached my position, and I told him what had happened. He crawled back for the medic, and when he reached to where I was, I told him the same, and he rolled over the dyke with the next round of shots. A good many of my friends were dead. I'd left my helmet on the other side of the dyke, along with a rucksack full of rations and so forth, thinking it would be easier to crawl without them, thinking I would return for them later. I crawled through the nippa palms at the edge of the field. The leaves reached out of the brush, twenty feet into the air. When I reached the corner of the jungle, my squad sergeant appeared behind me. We crawled together into the jungle, where the Vietcong were. The jungle would be our cover. I looked into the jungle at one of the Vietcong, and I could make out his features. He seemed to be trying to find something to shoot. I put my sights on him and I shot. Then I reached into my pocket for a grenade, and as I let go my rifle so I could pull the grenade, there was an explosion."

That was the last Naranjo remembers with any clarity. He recalls fisting the grenade in a depression by the dyke. He recalls feeling as though he were waiting to die. He recalls a priest administering last rites. He recalls being placed in a poncho and dragged across the field to a waiting Medivac chopper. He doesn't remember feeling any pain. He couldn't see anything, but he wasn't in pain. He considered the pain, however. He searched for it, worked to understand it, thought back to the sign on the bedroom door of his childhood: "Thrust against pain because pain is the purifier and the keeper of wisdom." He struggled to make sense of the noises all around. There was a gunship. It came in ahead of the Medivac, spraying the jungle out in front, clearing a path. There were four men dragging Naranjo in the poncho, shouting out words of encouragement, talking him through. They tossed him into the chopper, which didn't even touch down. It was hovering, swarming. Naranjo tried to keep talking to the medic, to stay awake, but he imagines now that he was drifting in and out.

He was taken to an evacuation hospital and continued to drift in and out there for the next day. There was extensive damage to his face, around his eyes mostly, and also to his upper right arm, from the shoulder down. He was afraid to talk to the doctors and nurses for what they might tell him. He overheard whispers of permanent blindness and amputation, and he guesses now that he put these prospects out of his mind. He wasn't ready to hear them. He still wasn't in any pain, was still mostly in shock, and he lay there in darkness, looking back on the last face he feared he would ever see, the face of that Vietcong in the rice field looking for someone to shoot.

When his condition stabilized, he was sent to an army hospital in Japan, where he would ask for that mound of water-based clay that would shape the rest of his life. From there, he was sent back to an army hospital in Denver, where he was finally reunited with his family. He had lost so much weight that his parents didn't recognize him; they made the trip from New Mexico and walked right past him.

From Denver, Naranjo went to the Western Blind Rehabilitation Center in Palo Alto, California. He stayed for nearly three months, learning to read Braille and to adjust to his new reality. He approached the fact of his blindness with resolve and acceptance. It was what it was. He had his despairing moments, he says, but, for the most part, he was okay with it. He couldn't see, but he could see his way to a future. He thought back to that first lump of clay at his hospital bedside in Japan, and allowed himself to feel whole. His counselor at the rehabilitation center wanted to send Naranjo back to school to finish his degree, but he wanted to sculpt. That was his plan, and it was within reach. The only obstacle was the rehabilitation center itself.

"They had a workshop set up down in the basement," he says, "and there was a guy behind the desk, and he handed me a strip of leather, wanting me to make a wallet or something. I told him I didn't want to make one, and he couldn't understand this. He said, 'Well, if you don't want to make one, the next person who comes down here won't want to make one, either.' I said, 'That's your problem, not mine.' The man went upstairs to consider this with his supervisor, and, after a while, he came back and pointed me to a loom. 'I don't want to weave,' I said. 'What do you want to do?' he asked. I answered that I'd like to work with wood. He sent me to the woodworking area, where he showed me a table saw and a cute little bench that had been constructed from a kit, and told me I could make one of those. He handed me three pieces of lumber and told me to get to it. 'I don't want to make a bench,' I said. I asked instead for a block of wood, a mallet, and a chisel. He said they didn't have anything like that in the workshop, but, by the next day, the man had spoken with his supervisor again and arranged for the necessary materials, and I had my block of wood, my mallet and my chisel. Finally, I was happy."

Naranjo determined to move into his own apartment in Santa Fe a little more than one year after the explosion. His father worried how he would find a place to live. His mother worried how he would take care of himself. So he called his sister and asked her to help, and together they found a suitable apartment. He hitchhiked back and forth to Taos a couple of times, about seventy miles each way, to visit his family. He resisted the idea of a seeing-eye dog, thinking he didn't really need one. He didn't see the point. Plus, he didn't want to have take care of it; either you're a dog person, or you're not, and you don't become a dog person simply because you've become blind. He bought a car instead—a 1968 gold Grand Prix. He couldn't see, but he could see that he needed a car. "I was a young man," he explains. "I was dating."

Soon, Naranjo consulted a local artist who taught him how to work in wax. His idea was to cast his pieces into bronze, and he knew that a bronze mold could be taken from anything. Wax, he knew, was extremely forgiving, and with his limited dexterity in his right hand, forgiving was something he needed. Early on in his rehabilitation, the bad arm was in a sling, and, over the years, he experimented with a certain kind of brace designed to extend and strengthen his fingers. After that, he tried another contraption with a rubber-band design. Eventually, he was able to hold some items with his hand and could use it to balance and position.

He went to work with the same tenacious joy he'd brought to those wind sprints he used to run with his brother. His very first show was held in the library of the VA hospital in Albuquerque. There was an article in the local newspaper. He sold his first piece in a Taos gallery in 1970. He began entering juried competitions alongside sighted artists. He didn't hide the fact that he was blind, but he didn't advertise it either, although

Michael Naranjo with his
sculpture Emergence.
Photo by Mary C. Fredenburgh

soon his reputation would precede him. He was "the artist who sees with his hands," after all. He sold more pieces, for more money, and began exhibiting his work in more prestigious galleries. He received commissions and awards and was appointed to advisory boards and festival committees.

The one constant in Naranjo's renewed life was his work, the touchstone was that first small lump of water-based clay. When he created, the rest of the world fell away. When his fingertips remembered what his eyes had once seen, he felt whole again. Fully. Truly.

Along the way, Naranjo met his wife Laurie, who would become his partner in every respect, helping him to design his first house and his first studio, and to deal with local foundries and galleries. Lately, their shared passion has been the setting up of "touchable" exhibits in museums of Naranjo's work around the country, an outgrowth of the artist's frustration at not being able to "see" legendary, great works of sculpture for himself. In Europe, for example, many museum curators open their doors and their collections to blind visitors, allowing them to experience pieces through touch, but, in America, he finds too often that he has to shame curators into it.

"It's gotten better in recent years," he says. "We've taken photos of me touching well-known pieces without gloves, and if we make copies of these pictures and send them to the museums ahead of time, explaining what it is we'd like to do, we can usually get it done."

He marvels at his unusual, "firsthand" perspective on art history. "I had seen documentary films on Michaelangelo's work when I could see," he recalls, "and there I was, invited in to touch his *David*. What an amazing honor." Indeed, Naranjo wept the first time he "saw" the *David*. It was coarse, he says, dappled with age. It had been stationed outdoors before it was moved inside, and it was rough to his touch, not smooth the way he expected. He felt the arm where it had been broken. He reached down to the right fist and noticed a small pebble. "Michaelangelo carved it so it's floating in there," he shares. "It floats free in his fist. You can move it if you stick your finger in there. Of course, you can't get it out, but that's something you'll never read about in any art history book, and I think about that and I take great pleasure in it.

"Is there anyone else who has ever lived who has ever touched so many of Michaelangelo's pieces, inch by inch, other than Michaelangelo himself?" he wonders. "Perhaps he had assistants on different pieces, but it's unlikely he had the same assistants for the run of his career. I think of all those pieces I've touched over the years, and it's an amazing thing."

Once, on a visit to the Church of St. Peter in Chains in Rome, Laurie's broken French got Naranjo an invitation to "see" Michaelangelo's *Moses*. There were other visitors to the chapel's museum area, but Naranjo stepped right up to the statue and touched it. "I put my hand out and touched his foot," he relates, "a sandaled foot, and I could feel the hair at the back of my neck stand up. I remembered the piece from the documentary and realized that if that was Moses' foot, the rest of him was way up there, and I asked Laurie to see if she could find me a chair that I might stand on. There were all these people around, and they were probably annoyed that I was in the way of the piece, in the way of their photo, but nobody said anything, and I was too overwhelmed to feel self-conscious about it, or rushed. Laurie indicated a ledge, where I might stand to reach higher still, so I took off my shoes and stood on that ledge and I was able to feel up to his forehead."

Naranjo hopes to bring that same sense of awe and wonder to students throughout New Mexico in a variety of ways. He recently established the Touched by Art Fund, a community foundation that seeks to bus children to museums in Santa Fe. "In the regular school budgets," he says, "there's money for one trip per child to a museum, and that's for their entire public school career, from kindergarten through grade twelve. Once. I find that incredibly sad. Art is our survival. Sculpture, symphonies, poetry. The exposure to the arts in some of our outlying areas is so minimal, we felt something had to be done about it."

He also gives lectures and workshops to area schools, churches, civic groups, and to similar groups across the country. He recalls one workshop he conducted with five blind students, ages fourteen to sixteen, thrown together to work on a sculpture. The finished piece was to be placed in the lobby of a new wing being built at their school. "These students had never sculpted before," Naranjo says, "and when we started out, I got them talking about blindness. I wanted to know if any of them had ever seen, which I thought would inform our choices about who would carve what section of the piece, and none of them had ever seen. They were all congenitally blind, and the curious thing is that none of them wished to see. This was their world, this was all they knew. And what I realized, after talking with them, was that I don't need to see again, either. I hadn't really thought about this before, until I met these students, at least not in such a concrete way.

"The world I last saw in 1968 was a lot different than the world I know today, but the beauty of it is that I don't need to see it to understand it. I'm sure there's a whole lot out there that I would love to see, but I would also have to look at the ugliness that's out there as well. The two go hand in hand, the good and the bad. This way, I can see what I want to see. And that's the interesting truth. After thirty-five years of being blind, I have no desire to see. None at all. This is my world. I've lived in it long enough, longer at this point than I lived in a sighted world. I like it here. I love my life. I love my family, my wife and beautiful daughters. When I reach out with my left hand to look at something, what the tips of my fingers feel, they really see. I have very good visual imagery; my wife and daughters are very descriptive because that's the way my life is. I listen to books on tape when I work. I love my work. Why change it? Why rock the boat? Why waste time on something that can't happen?"

In the picture he keeps of himself in memory, Michael Naranjo is not a young man. He is not disabled. He is not a soldier. The measure of this man is in the graceful lines of his work, in the ways he has lived his life as a husband and a father and a sculptor, in the energy he gives back to a world that has taken so much from him even as it has gifted him so much more.

Too Tough to Die

Frank Bigelow
U.S. Navy, World War Two

Frank Bigelow was born hard to kill, and he's spent his years living like he has to back it up.

During World War Two, Seaman Second Class Bigelow survived nearly three-and-a-half years in Japanese POW camps, during which he contracted malaria, dysentery, and yellow jaundice—all at the same time, all without benefit of medication or even the smallest creature comfort, like a bed or a blanket. He was shot at and beaten and tortured and, once, nearly beheaded. He witnessed unimaginable cruelty and endured unthinkable hardship. During his extended captivity, his weight dropped to ninety-five pounds, which, on a young man of six feet four inches, didn't amount to much more than skin and bones. On an oppressive work detail in a Japanese coal mine, he had his right ankle broken by a falling rock, and when the shattered bones refused to heal and gangrene set in, another American POW performed a makeshift amputation with a hacksaw and a razor blade. After the war, in what could have been a tragic accident, he drove his

car into the side of a train in the middle of a blizzard
and somehow walked away with only minor injuries.

These days, the threat looms in the form of an
untreatable melanoma; in June, 2003, doctors gave
Bigelow just a couple months to live, but Bigelow refuses to accept the prognosis. Besides, he thinks, he's beat-
en bigger enemies than cancer, and he likes his chances.
He doesn't much care for the long odds the doctors laid
out for him, but he likes his chances.

Bigelow, a big, round-faced man with big, round-
faced glasses and a big, rousing voice to match his features, reckons there's been some kind of guardian angel
watching out for him all these years—back, even, when
he was a little boy. At just twenty months old, he was
out in front of his house in Pleasant Lake, North Dakota, pitching rocks on the train tracks that ran along the
property. One of his three older brothers was meant to
be watching him, but he, apparently, didn't do a good
job of it. Pleasant Lake is such a small town it doesn't
even show up on most maps, and even in 1922 it was
small enough that a kid like Frank Bigelow knew the
name of the local railroad conductor. On that one afternoon, Old Joe LaFrance ran his Great Northern freight
train around the curve from the east of the Bigelow
place, chugging along at approximately eighty miles per
hour. Old Joe looked down the track from about a mile
off and saw a small figure he guessed was a dog. He
tooted his horn, but the damn thing wouldn't move. The
conductor had no idea that the figure that lay in his path
was a child, but he slammed on the brakes and slid the
engine and thirteen boxcars to the best stop he could

manage. Whatever it was that had been in his path, he feared he must have hit it something fierce, and he stepped from the engine and walked back gingerly toward the caboose, afraid of what he might find. And sure enough, beneath the caboose, there was little Frankie Bigelow, bloodied and still. Old Joe thought he'd killed him, and he ran toward the Bigelow house to fetch help.

"Evidently," Bigelow says, "I'd been hit by the cow-catcher, the grille at the front of the train. Got hit in the head pretty good. Still got the scar to show for it. The rest of them cars, they managed to clear me, I was so small. Old Joe collected my mother and took us to the hospital in the caboose."

Bigelow wasn't merely hit and run over by the Great Northern freight train—he was hit and run over *fourteen* times, once for each cab and the engine itself—and the local doctors began to prepare his mother for the worst. He'd suffered a massive concussion and head trauma, although by some confluence of miracles the rest of his little body was pretty much unscathed. Still, about the best the doctors could hope was for the child to hold on until his father arrived to say his goodbyes. Well, when Bigelow's father finally did arrive, little Frank was still holding on, and an old country doctor, Doc Sorenson, asked the senior Bigelow if he could try an experimental treatment that just might save the boy. Bigelow's father said he could try anything if he thought it stood a chance. Dr. Sorenson arranged for an emergency surgery and placed a metal plate in the child's head.

"My skull was so soft," Bigelow explains. "I was still just a baby, and they put these screws in there to hold everything together, and I wore that thing until I was about four years old. By that point, my head was growing, and I used to get these godawful headaches. Jesus Christ, I can still remember them. So they took out the plate and that was that."

The older brother who'd been left in charge got quite a talking to after that day on the railroad tracks, and, for the longest while, he held it over his little brother. But after all this time, all that's left of the drama is the still-deep scar on Frank Bigelow's forehead and the still-gripping story that accompanies it. "Takes a lot more than a damn train to slow me down," he says.

A lot more, indeed.

Bigelow came of age at the butt end of the Great Depression, and by the time he was through with high school, there wasn't much in the way of opportunity out in his part of North Dakota. His father ran a grain elevator until a fire destroyed the operation in 1936; he'd been carrying mail from the post office to the depot ever since, earning just shy of twenty dollars per month for his trouble. Bigelow's brothers skipped town as soon as they finished school—Jack and Charles were off to West Virginia, and Don went out west. There wasn't much to hold a young Frank Bigelow to another North Dakota winter. "I couldn't steal a job," he says, although from time to time he managed to borrow one. He landed a part-time gig driving a dump truck, and another closed-ended job helping to build seven miles of new road in Benson County.

Soon enough, the road was nearly finished, and a nineteen-year-old Bigelow found himself just north of Minot, home now to a big U.S. air base, with just thirteen dollars in his pocket and not a single prospect to his name. He was walking down the street with his best buddy, Andy Geibel, when they happened across a sign that said, Uncle Sam Wants You. Bigelow turned to Geibel and said, "By God, Andy, let's join."

And, by God, they did. Bigelow did, anyway. Geibel, at five feet three inches, didn't make the cut as far as the navy was concerned, but Bigelow signed on just the same, heading off to boot camp in Great Lakes, Illinois. He thought he'd seen the worst of what winter had to offer, growing up in North Dakota, but he'd never been to Great Lakes, Illinois. "Jesus Christ, it's awful," he says. "That has got to be the coldest place in the world, I think. By God, the way that wind comes off that lake, it'll kill ya."

That is, it might have killed a lesser spirit, but it couldn't touch Frank Bigelow, not really. He traded Illinois for his first duty on the USS *Arizona*, which was dry-docked in Bremerton, Washington. Bigelow stood fire watch on the ship for three months, while the *Arizona* was being refitted. He damn near froze to death, he says now. It was cold and wet and rainy and stinky, and one night on watch, Bigelow saw a sign posted on a message board looking for volunteers to ship out to the Philippines. He sought out the person in charge. "Is it warmer there in the Philippines?" he asked, and when the answer came back in the affirmative, he put his name down and called it a change of plan.

He also might have called it another stroke of luck to transfer off the USS *Arizona* before it was attacked at Pearl Harbor several months later.

In the Philippines, Bigelow was stationed on the USS *Canopis*, a "sub tender" charged with the care and safekeeping of twenty-eight submarines in the region. The ship was known as "Mama-san," and Bigelow served dutifully as a communications yeoman for the entire Second Division. He was especially pleased that he drew submarine pay, which amounted to an extra ten dollars per month, which was everything to Bigelow. He was even more thrilled with the setting. After a lifetime of brutal cold and harsh, dirt-patch summers, the Philippines was like a balm to Bigelow. He loved the land and the climate. He loved the Filipino people, especially after they were asked to stand up and fight. "The morning after they hit Pearl Harbor, they hit Manila," Bigelow recalls. "Wiped out all the ships in Manila Bay. The *Canopis*, we took one through the fantail, and it went through five decks and exploded in a shaft alley. Blew the main bearing off the screw shaft."

With some pluck and ingenuity, the ship's commander was able to ease the *Canopis* toward the southern tip of Bataan, into the harbor, and tie her to a stone quarry dock. "We were on fish nets from the main mast to the top of the hill," Bigelow relates. "Disguised her up real good. Put a bunch of leaves and stuff on it, and we were okay for about ten days. And then all those leaves turned brown, and you could see her from a hundred miles. And they really bombed us. Jesus Christ, they really bombed us."

Ultimately, the crew put the *Canopis* on a starboard list and painted big scratches on her hull, hoping to make it look like she'd been abandoned as derelict. Bigelow and company worked on the ship under cover of night and slept during the day in three tunnels they'd dug into the side of a mountain.

"We dug in like that for about five months," he reports, "and those Filipino scouts did more fighting that anybody else. Turned our 31st Infantry into a real fighting unit, when all these guys had ever done in their life was parade."

Five months into the ordeal, the men were down to third rations—and they weren't even getting those half the time. They ate snakes, caribou, anything they could find on that mountainside. A good percentage of the men contracted malaria. There was a hospital, but it had been shelled so many times the nurses made wards under the trees. The conditions were miserable, and, for a time, Bigelow thought their prospects were even worse.

"All we had to live on was hope," he says, "and it was false hope, you know, the way it turned out. They kept telling us that British Navy ships were coming in and all this bullshit, and we hung on. Fight to the last man, that was the message, and we were damn near down to the last man, I'll tell you that."

Bigelow was part of a team that made a month-long stand on the island fortress of Corregidor after the surrender at Bataan, including an epic battle on the beach with an air-cooled .50-caliber machine gun. Bigelow and another sailor were left to defend the beach, and they did a valiant job of it. "All I had to do was keep loading them for this fellow Havey," he recalls. "I had a pair of asbestos slugs, and I was changing barrels. Havey was firing. And it was just like shooting ducks in a barrel because of how the Japs were coming in, and because of our position. Must have wiped out two boatloads of 'em, and the ones that made it through cut right into our barbed wire. Jesus Christ, it was pitiful. But somehow, one of them got up onto the hill where we were firing, and Havey took about seven shots right across the chest. He was standing right next to me. He turned around and walked about ten steps and fell dead."

A few hours later, the American troops surrendered, and Bigelow was taken by his Japanese captors to an Allied airfield. Thousands of men, mostly Americans, were herded onto approximately twenty acres of concrete, left to survive against the elements, and made to watch as Japanese guards hauled down an American flag, ground it into the dirt, and took turns urinating on it. The scene left Bigelow feeling sickened and determined to overcome whatever came his way next, but that determination only took him so far. For the next ten days, the prisoners were given no food, no water, no medicine. Dozens of the men died on that airfield, and almost everyone developed malaria. Bigelow reports that he "damn near" died, once again.

From the airfield, the prisoners were loaded onto Japanese landing boats—fifty men per boat—and pushed out into approximately ten feet of water in the harbor protecting one of Manila's prestigious yacht clubs. Most of the men were able to swim to shore, but some were not. Once again on dry land, the prisoners were paraded through the streets of Manila—a heartless show of Japanese might over the American enemy. The prisoners hadn't eaten in more than ten days. They were sick and weak and wet and bone tired. Bigelow guesses that they looked pathetic, and yet in the eyes of the Filipino children lining the streets, they walked like heroes. The children knew how hard the men had fought, and they wanted to show their appreciation.

"The Japanese didn't want these kids to get near us," Bigelow remembers, his voice choked with fondness for the Filipino children and disdain for the Japanese guards patrolling the streets. "They were hitting at them with sticks and hitting at them with bayonets and hitting at them with everything they had. And them kids would keep charging that line, wanting to get to us with a cigarette or a leaf full of rice. Something. Or maybe it was just to shake our hands. And the Japs would hit at them with clubs and sticks. I seen one of them kill one kid. Just picked up his rifle and shot him. A little boy, not more than ten or twelve years old."

In Bigelow's estimation, the harsh treatment of the Filipinos must have fired up the American troops because men who'd been dragging suddenly picked up a step; where there had been no will to live, there was now resolve. At least, that's how Bigelow saw it, and he went from resignation to that same resolve on that long, dispiriting march. And yet, as it had been with the vile desecration of the American flag, his resolve wasn't enough; he was marched directly to a Manila prison, where he was kept for another three days without food.

From there, he was loaded onto a train with one hundred men per small French boxcar. "You couldn't fall down if you died," he says. "Jesus Christ, it was impossible to get air through them wooden walls. I had to pick a hole in the wall with a spoon, and I was able to get some fresh air. Otherwise, I wouldn't have made it. They kept us on that damn train for days and days."

The train let out at Cabantuan, only about thirty miles from Corregidor, but you'd never know it from all that time in those boxcars. From there, the Americans were marched to Camp Three, an outpost that originally had been built as barracks for the Filipino army, but never used and, probably, never finished. The prisoners were made to dig slit trenches for toilets. "It was the stink hole of the world," Bigelow says. "Walking around in feces up to your shoe tops. It was horrible."

This time, Bigelow became so sick he had to be removed from the general population to a small wooden building across the way known as the Death Ward. The accommodations there weren't any better than the main camp barracks, except that on the Death Ward, they didn't even pretend to feed you; they figured you were going to die anyway, so what was the point?

Bigelow had malaria, yellow jaundice, and dysentery all at the same time, and all were left to run their course, untreated. He lay still for the longest time on the hard wooden floor, wondering what it would be like to die, wondering if he might be better off. Someone had placed a pile of charcoal at his side, and, soon enough, he was drawn to it. When you haven't eaten in who-can-remember-how-long, you reach for whatever's near, even if whatever's near is a pile of charcoal. Bigelow leaned up on his elbows and choked down every last piece of the stuff, then rolled over again onto his back and waited to die. Everything turned gray. He began to drift. And then, for some reason, he turned a kind of corner. He doesn't know if it was the charcoal or a shift in perspective. He said to himself, "Bigelow, you're too young to die." He actually said the words out loud. Then he raised himself back up on his elbows, struggled to his feet, and walked slowly back across the road to the main barracks. He wasn't feeling any better, not yet, but there was a will to live in place of no will at all.

Later, the Japanese transferred a few of the sickest prisoners from the main barracks to a hospital camp, and Bigelow was moved with this group. "Wasn't much of a hospital," Bigelow tells. "Not like they had medicine or anything. A doctor might come around and see you, or he might not. At some point, I was given some liquid quinine. You talk about some awful shit to drink. Jesus Christ. But it seemed to do the trick. That or the charcoal or some combination of both, I think."

After three weeks in the hospital camp, Bigelow was up and around and moving with the other prisoners. Whatever it was had passed. He was down to ninety-five pounds, and he wasn't likely to survive another illness in his weakened condition, but for the time being, he was all right.

Back in the main barracks again, Bigelow met with a welcome surprise—a friendly face from home. He was standing in line one day, hoping to get a little extra rice, and he heard a familiar voice holler his name. He'd have recognized that voice anywhere: Ray Eurquart. He and Bigelow used to run with sisters together back in North Dakota, that's how close they'd been, all through high school, making more trouble than you could throw a book at. And here he was, half a world a way, in this stink hole of a prison camp at Cabantuan. What were the odds? As it turned out, Ray had joined the army and been captured in the southern Philippines some months earlier. Ray caught a break, too, after his capture. He was plucked from the line by a Japanese officer and put to work driving his car. He lived pretty decently for about three months, until the officer was reassigned, and Ray was thrown back in with the rest of the prisoners and eventually moved to Cabantuan.

The first morning after the two friends from North Dakota were reunited, Eurquart pulled a grueling burial detail. Some overweight Japanese sergeant had succumbed to Beri-beri, and while Eurquart was lugging the three-hundred-pound body into its just-dug grave, he stepped in a hole and threw his back out. All of a sudden, he couldn't work. Hell, he could barely move, and he wouldn't eat. They took him over to the hospital camp, and he was given a little rice, a little seaweed soup, enough to get by. But Eurquart wouldn't eat a thing. Bigelow fetched his buddy's rations and tried to feed them to him, but Eurquart refused all food. After a week and a half or so, Bigelow could see what his old friend was up to.

"He was committing suicide, was what it was," he explains. "I picked him up in my arms and said, 'Ray, I know what you're doing.' And he said, 'Biggie, I just can't make it.' I told him, I said, 'I'm going home and tell your dad that you were the yellowest son of a bitch ever come down that road.' At first, he raised up a bit, as if he was trying to hit me, but then he set back down. So I said it again, about three more times, until finally he said, 'Biggie, it's no use. I know what you're doing, but it's no use.' And he died right there in my arms. Just like that. Eleven days into that hell hole. He'd been clean and healthy and eating pretty good, driving for that Japanese officer. Out in the fresh air all the time. And then to walk into that godawful place. We'd come up through it, you know. We'd learned to live with it. But it was just too much for Ray. Too much for a lot of them guys."

Bigelow was put to work as soon as he was well enough to move around, detailed to Bataan where he and approximately one hundred other prisoners cleaned and sorted the scrap metal from the American trucks and tanks and airplanes that had been left behind. It was arduous, excruciating, relentless work. Bigelow tells how the Japanese were so tight for supplies that they'd have the work crew drain the oil from the engines before sending them out for scrap. The prisoners were supposed to work eleven days straight, with a day off on the twelfth, but for some reason, that twelfth day never came around on the calendar—and on the few occasions when it did, it passed so quickly it didn't seem to matter.

By dumb luck, Bigelow was shifted from scrap detail and put to work driving a military police vehicle for a Japanese officer, and, for a stretch of time, he enjoyed slightly better treatment. Bigelow reports that the officer was actually fond of him because he drove fast and somewhat recklessly, but one afternoon he careened onto an overpass bridge and into a hairpin turn and noticed a baby sitting right in the middle of the road. In a flash, his mind was back in North Dakota on those Great Northern train tracks out by his house, and he was Old Joe LaFrance, doing what he could to steer clear. "I cut the wheel real quick," he says. "It was automatic. And next thing I knew, we were flipping over into a telephone poll—tore the side off the car and through that Jap officer out onto a rice paddy. Landed right on his head. Didn't hurt him, though. Didn't hurt the baby, either, and that was the point, but that night the officer called me in. And he understood what had happened. And he said, 'In America, you miss the baby. Here, we hit the baby.' And that was about the size of it, too. And he wouldn't let me drive for him anymore."

Eventually, Bigelow was shipped to Japan with hundreds of other prisoners to a camp in Omuta, across the harbor from Nagasaki. It was Camp Seventeen, the site of one of the tragic, under-reported stories of World War Two, and Bigelow's base of operations for a while. There, he was put to work in an abandoned coal mine that was owned and operated by the Mitsui Mining Corporation. The mine hadn't been worked in more than ten years. It had been "worked out," in miners' parlance, meaning there was no longer enough in the way of resources to justify the increasing risk as the supporting structure became more and more compromised. This, of course, had been of great concern to a Japanese corporation when it had been charged with the well-being of its employees—and the mine had indeed been closed because of hazardous working conditions—but it was of no concern at all when there were able-bodied American and Allied prisoners available in Camp Seventeen to do the same work. The Americans were put to work "pulling pillars"—removing the safety pillars that had been put in place to protect the miners in their initial task. Typically, these pillars were written off as part of the cost of such dangerous business, but the Japanese were in desperate need of coal, and it was thought another push into these mines might yield some surplus coal and that the pillars could be put to good use in opening other mines.

"It was probably the most dangerous job in the world," Bigelow says, perhaps without exaggeration. "Luckily, we had a couple of pretty good Jap guards, men who'd done some of this same work themselves, who showed us how to stay alive. How you could put your hand on the ceiling and feel the vibration and tell within ten seconds if the thing was coming down."

Month after month, Bigelow cheated death on this mining detail, working at the very bottom of the mine, sixteen levels down. The Americans came up with all kinds of ways to stall or diminish the workload, but they still had to go through the motions. They still had to stop in the Buddha room and bow to Buddha before entering the mine. ("Hell," Bigelow figures, "after we'd been in there one time, we'd have bowed to anybody.")

They still had to strip down to their underwear to work in the mine, leaving their clothes in the Buddha room. They still had to make that long trek down through all those perilous levels, eleven days on with one day off, except during *taksanshigoto*, which meant there was to be no rest at all; at one point, Bigelow and company worked twenty-seven days in a row.

The detail lasted for nearly two years, during which the prisoners were routinely beaten, often for no reason at all. Once, in a fit of pique and misguided frustration, Bigelow threw a rock at a company guard. He says now that he never meant to hit the guard, only to release some anger, but the guard turned him in. Bigelow was badly beaten by an American-educated Japanese soldier who had apparently taken a liking to him. You would not have known it for the man's actions. "He beat the crap out of me with his fists," Bigelow says, "and I refused to go down, but he kept beating me until I did. I'd seen them cut the heads off other prisoners for far less than throwing a rock, so I thought I was in for it, but after I went down, he backed off. He was done. Next day, the fella comes down with an extra *bento* box—the lunch boxes they had—and he gave it to me and apologized for having to hit me like that. Said if he hadn't, they'd have cut my head off, like they done those other times. Said with the beating he'd given me, that was enough."

Bigelow returned to work the next day and made a better effort at controlling his temper, but there was a great deal that went on in those mines that remained out of his control. One day at Christmastime in 1944,

Bigelow noticed a big boulder spring loose and start for him. It registered that the rock was headed his way, but he was powerless to do anything about it. He was weak from malnutrition and the oppressive work detail, and his reaction time wasn't what it was back before he'd been captured. By the time he tried to run from the boulder's path, it was too late. The rock caught his right ankle and just about broke it straight off. His bones were so brittle they snapped like dead twigs. Four American prisoners slapped him on a loose board and dragged him up six levels to where they could load him on a coal car to take him topside.

There, they took Bigelow to the Buddha room, where it must have been approximately thirty degrees. He was dressed, still, in only his underwear, so his friends grabbed at the clothes that had been left behind by the other prisoners and draped them across Bigelow's body to keep him warm. The Japanese guards made the prisoners return to work once Bigelow was settled, and he was left to lay there in that frigid room for hours. Later, Dr. Thomas Hewlett, another POW, told Bigelow that the cold kept him alive. Otherwise, he would have bled to death.

For the longest time, Dr. Hewlett worked to reset Bigelow's ankle, but the bones were fairly shattered and there were no medical supplies. The doctor tried to fashion a splint from an old bicycle spoke, hoping to thread the thing through Bigelow's ankle to hold the bones together, but the primitive contraption proved useless. Eventually, they loaded Bigelow onto the back of a three-wheel motorcycle and transported him back to camp, where his condition deteriorated. Dr. Hewlett became concerned about gangrene and told Bigelow he would have to remove the right leg. Bigelow told him to go ahead and take it. He was ready for anything. He had steeled himself against this eventuality. Lying there in that Buddha room, cold and alone, an amputation seemed inevitable. It was not a thing he relished, but it was a thing he had to face. There was no medication. No whiskey. No nothing. Just a hacksaw, a razor blade, four guys to hold Bigelow down, and a fifth guy to knock him out with a punch to the jaw.

"I'll never forget when he first started to cut," Bigelow tells. "I said, 'Doc, you've got to give me something. A drink of whiskey, an aspirin tablet. Something.' And he said, 'Biggie, if I had anything, I'd take it myself.' God, he was something."

To prevent infection, Dr. Hewlett resorted to another primitive technique. He placed maggots inside the wound before applying the bandages, hoping the maggots would eat away at any contagion. He didn't tell Bigelow about this part of the procedure, however, and three or four days after the operation, Bigelow felt a weird sensation where his leg used to be. "He took the bandages off," Bigelow says, "and pulled out a whole bunch of maggots, and I damn near fainted, but they saved my life."

When he was well enough to move around, the guards threw a pair of Japanese crutches at Bigelow and ordered him back to work, but he was spared any trips back into that mine. Instead, he was assigned the job of making straw shoes for the miners—ten each day—and he never failed to meet his quota, on into the summer of 1945.

All during this time, news from the outside world made its way into Camp Seventeen by radio or by word-of-mouth, and the mood of the prisoners lifted as Allied bombers began to fill the skies over Japan. Bigelow remembers the men praying for those pilots to drop their bombs right on top of them, remembers thinking it strange to wish for a direct hit, but remembers also the certainty that those bombs would put an end to their misery, one way or another.

"When they finally dropped the big boy on Nagasaki, we didn't hear it," Bigelow says. "There was so damn much bombing going on, up close, fire bombs, about half our camp already burned down, that we just didn't hear it. Wasn't till the next morning, I come up out of a hole with my friend Billy Gunner and we saw that great big cloud off in the distance. He turned to me and said, 'Jesus Christ, Biggie, they must have dropped a thousand-pounder over there.' Sure enough, it was the biggest cloud we'd ever seen. And a thousand pounds? That was about the biggest thing we'd ever heard of, and, at that time, we didn't know a thing about any atomic bomb. Never heard of it. Wasn't until a week or so later, some war correspondent came through our camp in a jeep, filled us in on what had happened."

His days as a slave laborer finally over, Bigelow looked ahead to a lifetime of uncertainty. About the only thing he knew was that he would somehow find his way. After everything he'd been through, how could he not?

From Omuta, he went by train to Nagasaki and witnessed firsthand the devastation in the industrial district. The rubble. The brown masses of rust. The smell of death in the air still. There was a navy hospital ship set to take him and some of the other prisoners to Okinawa, and as the train pulled into the station and all the other men scrambled to disembark, Bigelow held back. He couldn't run. All he had were those lousy Japanese crutches, and he'd never quite figured them out. He had his window open, leaned out, and spied a navy nurse on the platform—the first American woman he'd seen in four years. He hollered down to her. "Baby," he said, "can you catch me?"

The nurse held out her arms and said, "Come on!"

Bigelow jumped and landed square in her arms. If he'd weighed any more, he would have landed on his rear, but he'd barely eaten in two years.

He looked up at the nurse and said, "Can I kiss you?"

And she looked down and said, "Honey, you can do any goddamn thing you want."

And so, he kissed her.

The hospital ship survived a perilous hurricane en route to Okinawa, but Bigelow eventually made it to Guam, and then on to San Francisco, where the first thing he did was drop to his knees and kiss the ground. The second thing he did was call home to North Dakota; he had to chase all those neighbor women off the party line so his mother could actually hear him. His mother said she knew he was all right. Deep down, she knew. After what had happened to him as a child, she said there was an angel looking out for him. Bigelow liked to agree.

Two of his brothers drove clear across the country from Maryland to meet up with Bigelow at the naval hospital in Oakland. "Fifty-four hours, on them old roads," he marvels. "They had them a '41 Pontiac, and I don't think they clocked less than a hundred miles an hour the whole way there. Then we drove up to Oregon to get my brother Don, and the four of us were together again, first time in fifteen years."

Bigelow was twenty-four years old, and he had no clear path he felt he was meant to follow. There were still some follow-up surgeries and a long rehabilitation stint at the Philadelphia Naval Hospital, but for the first time since he was taken prisoner, he started to think about what he might do with the rest of his life. For the life of him, he couldn't hit on a workable plan. He drove a taxi for a time, and then he bought into a cab business in the Washington, D.C. area. He made a good go of that, then a job as an ad salesman for a local newspaper looked a little more promising. And it was, until the publisher went bankrupt. He signed on with another newspaper as circulation manager, sold Fords for a while, then somehow landed as a salesman for a propane gas company.

It was during this period that Bigelow ran his car into the sidecar of a moving train during a whiteout snowstorm, and he walked away from his second near-fatal train wreck wondering if his number would ever be called.

Underneath the various stops and starts and the now-familiar brushes with death was the effort that would sustain Frank Bigelow for the next half-century. In 1947, along with other survivors of the Japanese prison camps, Bigelow signed on to a massive legal claim seeking reparations for their harsh, cruel treatment as slave laborers in the "employ" of several major Japanese corporations, including Mitsui, Mitsubishi, and Nippon Steel. Indeed, in February, 1951, Bigelow became the very first American veteran of World War Two to receive a government check as compensation for his time in the Japanese POW camps; the money came from a pool of assets seized from Japan and Germany at the end of the war. The price placed on three-and-a-half years in captivity: $1,198—one dollar for each day Bigelow spent as prisoner. At the time, it was enough to pay off the loan on a new cab, but Bigelow figures it doesn't come close to what he is owed. "They owe me a leg," he calculates. "They owe me three years of my life. They owe me miner's wages for the work I did for them. And they owe me a goddamn apology."

He means to get his due. Bigelow has been out in front as the national commander of the American Defenders of Bataan and Corregidor (ADBC), and as one of the most outspoken critics against Japan's treatment of its prisoners. Some years after the dollar-per-day award offered in 1951, the courts determined that the figure be raised to one hundred dollars per day, but the matter is still pending. Recently, the ADBC threw in with a new team of lawyers in San Diego and Atlanta,

Frank Bigelow

who hope to take the case all the way to the U.S. Supreme Court—and Bigelow likes his chances.

Lately, though, his worries are more personal in nature. With a diagnosis of skin cancer, Frank Bigelow has traded the big picture for a much smaller one, and his focus is on hanging on and beating his prognosis into the ground. He has his reasons. Back in 2002, he met his wife Charlene on a blind date, and now his goal is to make it to his one-year wedding anniversary. His reasons are more practical than romantic. "She's the best thing that ever happened to me," he says. Indeed, a visit to his comfortable home in Brooksville, Florida, underlines the sentiment. Charlene administers his

medications, changes his bedpan, coordinates his benefits, argues with the phone company, and keeps him
generally comfortable, well-fed, and happy. Bigelow
means to repay her many kindnesses in what ways he
can. If he makes it to their first anniversary, Charlene
will be eligible for his full service benefits—and to
Bigelow right now, that deadline is everything. To have
survived two train wrecks and three-and-a-half years in
those Japanese prison camps, with various bouts of
malaria, dysentery, jaundice, and gangrene mixed in for
good measure, only to fall victim to an inoperable
tumor in his groin that's cutting off circulation to his
stomach. . . . Well, it hardly seems fair to check out
before ensuring that his doting new wife will be taken
care of when he's gone. Bigelow refuses to let that happen, and he's calling on that same measure of resolve
and determination that saw him through those hardships in Omuta to see him through one time more.

*Authors' note: After a long lifetime of cheating death
and beating the variously long odds against him, Frank
Bigelow lost his battle to cancer in the summer of 2003.*

THE SILENT ENEMY

Felecia Weston
U.S. Army, Persian Gulf War

To listen to former Signal Corps Specialist Felecia Weston talk of the October, 1990 SCUD missile launched on a U.S. Army base in Dhahran, Saudi Arabia, is to hear the voice of fear and guilt and killing uncertainty. Even now, more than a decade removed from the blast, and following another full-scale engagement against Saddam Hussein's Iraqi forces, Weston is moved to tears and confusion when recalling the attack and its aftermath—tears for the lives lost in the explosion and confusion over the haunting fact that her life was spared.

"There's not a day goes by," she says haltingly, "when I don't see myself back at that base, wandering around in that rubble, trying to figure out what happened. Not a day goes by without me struggling to make sense over why I survived and all those other people did not."

The explosion, which claimed the lives of twenty-eight American and Allied servicemen and women and injured ninety-eight more, carried a compelling footnote to recent military history. It was the final SCUD missile attack before the cease-fire the following day that put an effective end to Operation Desert Storm. It was launched by an enemy that would continue to threaten U.S. interests until the second Iraqi war in 2003. As such, it was a last-gasp reminder to Allied forces in the Persian Gulf that the world had not seen the last of Saddam Hussein and his terrorist regime, but to Weston, the blast continues to resonate on a much more personal level. She suffers from intense, relentless migraine headaches and a crippling survivor's guilt that has left her feeling clinically depressed and emotionally drained. There's a sadness, too, that she seems to carry like a weight she'd rather shed.

"Sometimes I think I'd be better able to deal with what happened if I'd lost a limb, or an eye," she says, suggesting that if there were some tangible, physical evidence of her ordeal, she might be better able to hide behind it or move past it. It is a moving, unflinching admission from someone who has given valiantly to her country—the only member of her battalion to receive a Purple Heart for the wounds she suffered in the attack. Weston suffered irreparable damage to one eye, leaving her vision permanently blurred and causing intense migraines—conditions that have deteriorated in the intervening years and will likely worsen with age. Still, she says, "I don't feel I gave enough. I feel people are looking at me all the time, and judging me, and thinking, how is it that this girl managed to survive? Why her? I feel as though, if I was gonna make it out of there, there should have been more of a sacrifice."

Weston speaks with the soft, swallowed-up voice of someone who doesn't want to make too much noise or say the wrong thing. She's thought about the explosion a great deal; indeed, at times, it seems it's all she thinks about—or, she thinks about *not* thinking about it, which in the end amounts to the same thing. She contrasts the way she is now—quiet, reserved, aloof—with the ways she used to be before enlisting—boisterous, outgoing, social—and she can't recognize the girl she was beneath the woman she has become. And the changes run deeper than aspects of personality; there's been a physical transformation, too. She's less energetic, she says, less able to push herself, less likely to accept a challenge or set a far-off goal.

Lately, Weston works as a national service officer for the Disabled American Veterans office in Waco, Texas, fulfilling a commitment she made to herself as she lay on a stretcher in a MASH unit in Dhahran, her eyes wrapped in bandages and her imagination running to permanent blindness and the final horrifying images she feared might be the last she would ever see. The headaches had not yet started, but she was already feeling the stress and strain of what she had seen and heard. All of those bodies. All of those cries for help. All of that confusion and terror. She wanted to give something back if she made it out whole, and after a second tour of duty and an unlikely (and unwelcome) return to Saudi Arabia, she is finally doing just that. The work is everything to her—helping veterans to negotiate their way through paperwork and policy in order to claim the benefits to which they're entitled—and yet she continues to be haunted by the SCUD missile attack and the mixed blessings of having survived it.

Weston was something of an army brat growing up. She was born in Karlsruhe, Germany, where her father was stationed. For a time, she lived surrounded by families that never stayed in one place for too long, individuals who never had to take the time to make real, lasting, personal connections. After her parents divorced and her mother remarried another serviceman, she knew full well what it was to live with the complex uncertainties of a life in the military. She never meant to embrace that life for herself, but it came calling just the same. She'd attended a community college in Texas and had begun a career in retail sales when a cousin suggested that the two of them join the army together. To hear Weston tell it, the suggestion came in the form of a dare, and she rose to meet it.

"I was kind of bored with what I was doing," she says, "and my cousin put it out there, and she didn't like what she was doing either, and it seemed like a good enough idea at the time." At the time, in the fall of 1987, army recruiting officers were promoting a "buddy system," which encouraged friends to throw in together with the promise of serving together. Weston and her cousin allowed the idea to take hold, and the next thing they knew, they'd enlisted. As it happened, she and her cousin didn't even make it to basic training together. "So much for the buddy system," she says, but she had gotten her mind around the idea of service, so it didn't much matter if her cousin was at her side. What mattered was the good work she would do on behalf of her country, the sense of pride and purpose for which she found she was longing, and the adventure that lay ahead.

In Weston's mind, that adventure was never meant to include combat. In 1987, Weston's take on the global picture was that she could serve her four years in relative peace. There were no hot spots to which she thought she might be sent, no front lines where she might have to point a weapon in battle or have a weapon pointed at her. "I don't know that I would have gone, if it had been a different time in our history," she admits. "Honestly, that wasn't what it was about for me, the fighting, the putting your life on the line. What it was about was lifting myself from whatever path I was on and setting down on another one. Making a difference, but making a difference behind the scenes."

That behind-the-scenes perspective soon shifted to front and center. Weston's first duty assignment was in Germany, not far from where she'd been born, so she felt like she'd come full circle. From there, she was assigned to Charlie Company 67 as a multi-channel communications operator, based initially in Fort Gordon, Georgia. She never meant to work in communications, but it turned out to be something she was good at, something she enjoyed, and when Operation Desert Storm was declared she was sent with her unit to Saudi Arabia to establish communications systems there. She moved around a lot, Weston recalls, and was separated from her company, going wherever a new line needed to be established. With each move, she was reminded of the disconnect she used to know as a child, never stopping long enough in any one place to build real relationships.

On October 31, 1990, she was in Dhahran, helping to lay in a communications system for a large oil company, working twelve-hour shifts alongside the 475th Quartermaster Group, which had just been assigned to the same compound. Again, Weston recalls feeling out of sorts because all these new people had just arrived at the same time, and she was still learning who everyone was, trying to keep their assignments straight, and attaching names to faces. The mood in the compound was generally upbeat; after a weeks-long display of overpowering American force and fortitude, a cease-fire appeared imminent—but, still, the fighting continued. At just after eight PM, Weston returned to her barracks following her shift. She took off her BDU—battle dress uniform—jacket and began to change her clothes. There'd just been an inspection that morning, so her wall locker was locked. She was fiddling with her keys when, for some reason, she crossed to a nearby window. At about the same moment, she began to hear sirens, but didn't pay too much attention to them because she was always hearing sirens. They were like background music during her time there because they went off constantly, and the first peals were sometimes ignored.

Just as she looked out the window, the glass shattered and blew into the room with tremendous force. There was a black cloud of smoke. Weston screamed as she closed her eyes to the spray of glass and fumes. When she opened them, a beat or two later, she could see out of only one eye, and what she saw fairly terrified her. People running around and screaming. People bleeding. People dying. Outside, through where the window used to be, she could see a tremendous amount of smoke. Her face had been cut by the window glass and she was gushing blood, but she didn't know she was bleeding until someone told her. She doesn't recall feeling any pain or thinking to check for wounds or injuries. Her first proactive thought was to locate her gas mask. She had no idea what had caused the explosion or what, in fact, had exploded, and she wanted to cover all possibilities. She located her mask and struggled to put it on, but she couldn't get it to seal, so she gave up trying. There was commotion of every stripe. The sirens continued to wail. There were shouts of agony, shouts of confusion, shouts of instruction.

"I don't care how much you talk about something like this," Weston says. "I don't care how prepared you are. When it actually happens, it's a different story. Everybody was running around all over the place. Nobody knew what was happening. Nobody knew what to do next."

Somehow, American PATRIOT missiles had failed to intercept an Iraqi SCUD missile that had been launched at the Dhahran compound. The apparent target had been an ammunitions warehouse located approximately fifty yards from Weston's cinder block barracks. As she spilled from her barracks, she was directed back toward the side of the building, away from the warehouse, where small arms ammunition had already begun firing on their own, detonated by the explosion. Weston did as she was instructed, and when she felt she had reached safety, she looked across at the site of the blast in time to witness a second blast. The missile had been split, and the second explosion followed the first by about a minute. There was a flash of hot, bright light and a thundering boom. That time, the entire warehouse was destroyed.

"I felt so alone," she says, "watching what was happening. By this point, I knew I'd been hurt, but I just wanted to find someone from my company. That was the most important thing to me. There were only three of us there to begin with, three to a shift, but I didn't know any of these other people. I hit the ground. We all hit the ground, and I lay there thinking, I have to find someone I know."

Soon, Weston was ushered beyond the compound to a waiting vehicle to be driven to the nearest MASH unit. The windows in the vehicle had all been shattered in the explosion, and she sat on crushed glass all the way to the hospital. There was a guy next to her screaming that he couldn't feel his legs, and a young woman with a huge wedge of glass stuck in her neck, looking like she'd been shot with a glass arrow. Weston could only see from her one good eye, and even that one wasn't so good. The images were blurry and confusing, and she guesses now that this had as much to do with the shock of the moment and the general chaos all around as it did with any short-term damage.

There was a radio playing in the hospital, and Weston picked up bits and pieces of what had happened. She heard a number attached to the casualties. She heard the official American response. She heard various explanations and theories for the apparent failure of the PATRIOT missile system. She had been right in the middle of it, but it was only from her stretcher in the hospital that she was able to get any perspective on the attack. Both eyes were bandaged, and she lay there in darkness, accepting the kindness of the two medical officers assigned to her treatment. It's going to be okay, they took turns telling Weston, but she didn't accept that things would be okay. She broke down and cried. It was because of this kindness that Weston made that pledge to devote her life to helping other veterans. Really, she thought, these people didn't have to sit with her, comfort her, and offer these gentle reassurances; these particular compassions were above and beyond the call of duty, and she vowed to give back something of the same, someday, somewhere.

And yet even with the kind attention of these medical officers, Weston felt terribly, hopelessly alone. She was used to talking to her mother several times per week on the telephone—one of the great perks of being a communications specialist—but here in the hospital, she couldn't even reach out long distance to anyone she knew. She determined to leave the hospital, to go back to her barracks, to find the rest of her unit. That was her place, she felt, where she needed to be. The doctors had taken the bandages off of her good eye, and she could see well enough. She didn't think there was anything more those good people could do for her. Everybody in the hospital told Weston she wasn't ready to leave, but she would not be put off, so somebody sent for her nearest commanding officer. He came and escorted Weston back to her unit. She couldn't stand the thought of spending the night in the hospital after what had happened. She wanted to be with people she knew, and that was the best she could do.

The whole way back to the compound, Weston kept reliving the explosion in her mind. The sounds, the smells, the emotions. It was a scene she'd replay every day in one way or another, a moment she could never chase from her thinking. She couldn't think how it was that she had managed to survive. She kept dwelling on *what if?* scenarios, asking herself, what if I had been standing two feet to the left? What if I looked out the window a fraction of a second sooner? What if I'd gone directly to my bunk to lay down?

When she returned to the base, she saw soldiers and rescue workers hoisting bodies zipped into sleeping bags, one on top of the other. It had been just after eight o'clock in the morning when the missile hit, just after a change of shift. A lot of people were already back in their bunks by the time of that first explosion, and here they were being tossed in a giant pile.

The first thing Weston did when she returned to the unit was call home. Her mother heard something in her voice right away. "What's wrong?" her mother asked.

"Well," Weston said. "We got hit."

"What do you mean you got hit?" her mother wanted know.

Weston told her, and her mother was floored. "Oh my God," she said, back home in Texas, and then Weston's mother told her to pray. "Baby, get on your knees and start praying," she said.

Her mother was frantic with worry and wouldn't hear straightaway that her daughter was mostly okay.

Weston, in turn, caught her mother's worries and made them her own.

"She was making me so nervous," Weston says now, "telling me to get down and pray, that everything is gonna be okay. Only thing I could do was hang up the phone. I feel bad about that now, but I had to cut those thoughts right out of my head. I was having enough trouble dealing with what happened without my mother making it worse."

Later on that first night and into the next morning, Weston lay mostly awake on a bunk bed in a curtained-off section of the barracks. There was an A7, a sergeant first-class, assigned to the other bunk to keep her company, and she tried to keep Weston calm as best she could, but Weston recalls that she wasn't the best patient in military history. She jumped at every noise, every bump in the night. She heard the echoes of those cries of pain and terror. She saw the pile of sleeping bags. It was to be the first restless night of an endless string.

The next morning, when news of the cease-fire came across the radio, Weston was startled once again by the screams all around, but that time what she heard was screams of joy and exaggerated sighs of relief, rather than shrieks of terror. She heard the commotion and thought to herself, oh my God, not again. Please God, not again!

Now, nearly thirteen years after the SCUD missile attack, Weston continues to struggle. She never lost the vision in her left eye, but it has blurred with the years and will only get worse. She desperately needs glasses, but she refuses to wear them. More troubling, she says, is the constant pain and pressure she feels behind that left eye, the source of the migraine headaches that have plagued her since the explosions. Most troubling of all, though, is the survivor's guilt and the post traumatic stress disorder she's been wrestling with all these years. For the longest time, she didn't have a name for the various terrors and depressions that kept her up nights, but she eventually received a diagnosis and has been undergoing appropriate treatment ever since.

"In the beginning," she recalls, "they had me in group therapy with a whole bunch of Vietnam veterans, combat veterans. They were all struggling with some of the same issues, but I couldn't connect to these people. For one thing, I was the only woman in the group, but for another, they were all much older than me, and they'd all been in combat, and what they were dealing with might have appeared the same on paper, but in reality, it was a whole different thing. I don't think I said a word the entire time I was in that group."

Curiously—and courageously—Weston re-upped for another four years after her initial tour was through. She wound up staying in Dhahran for several months following the cease-fire, eventually resuming full activity after her wounds had healed. By the time she came home, she'd realized that her place was still in the service. "That was my life at that point," she explains. "It was all I knew." She also makes room for the notion that she re-enlisted as a way to give something back, to pay off an imagined debt for the fact of her survival and the care and benefits she'd received while recuperating.

Once again, she traveled the globe with her communications team, alighting in far-off places and close
to home. A few years into the second tour, she received
her orders for another assignment in Saudi Arabia. The
prospect loomed as the most daunting of her military
career: she was to return to the site of her endless
ordeal, in the company of a PATRIOT missile unit
whose mission had been to thwart the Iraqi SCUDs
during Operation Desert Storm. The irony was not lost
on Weston. She was being deployed as part of a team to
protect the airport, and as her group made ready, it
occurred to Weston that some of the men and women
she'd be working with would have been part of the
PATRIOT teams that missed that final SCUD. It was,
she felt, more than she could handle, such in-your-face
proximity to a moment she feared she would never
shake. She tried to get reassigned, but there was no
changing the orders.

She served her second assignment in Saudi Arabia
without specific incident, although she reports feeling
more restless during that time, more uncertain, more
afraid than ever before. "Frankly, I was a nervous
wreck," she admits, "and when my second tour was
finally up, in August, 1997, I decided it was time to get
out. Everything had just gotten so crazy. The survivor's
guilt, or what I now know was the survivor's guilt. The
stress. It was all just too much."

Weston took a job with the VA in Waco, Texas, not
far from her hometown, thinking she would finally fulfill
that pledge she'd made to herself on that hospital stretcher back in Dhahran, but she quickly grew frustrated with

the job. She'd thought she'd have a chance to work with veterans one-on-one to make more of a difference in their civilian lives, to give something back. Instead, she found herself pushing papers and punching a clock and scrabbling under the weight of military bureaucracy. Frustrated, she met someone at the DAV field office in the same building, where there happened to be an opening. She thought perhaps that job would be a better fit, and she grabbed at it when it was offered.

Now, six years later, she looks up from her desk at the DAV office in Waco and can't imagine how many lives she's touched through her work, how many broken families she's helped knit back together, how many first homes she's helped her clients find ways to finance.

Felecia Weston

With each victory, there's been a kind of refueling that keeps Weston going from one day to the next.

She still suffers from a nagging depression and a sense of guilt. She still suffers mightily with the migraines she will likely have to endure for the rest of her life. She still avoids the corrective eyewear she knows needs and dreads the day when her left eye fails her altogether. She's replaced the camaraderie of her time in the service with the familiarity of her hometown neighbors and tries to forget the fact that, outside the office, she is largely alone. She remembers how she was before enlisting that first time—fun-loving, happy-go-lucky, the kind of girl who'd string along three boyfriends at a time and never worry one would find out about another. She contrasts these memories with her present self—anxious, mistrustful, the kind of woman who'd rather load up on videos for a weekend of horror movies and action flicks than risk making a personal connection. She doesn't date. She doesn't socialize. Beyond her few friends at work, she keeps to herself and to her routines.

"There was one client," she recalls, "this one guy, and he was like a male version of me. Really, he was just like me. It was the strangest thing. I mean, I was sitting there on the phone with him, and we got to talking, discussing his case and everything, and his whole life sounded just like my life. The survivor's guilt, the feeling like he hadn't done enough, like he couldn't be in a relationship because of everything that had happened to him. And we just clicked, me and this guy. He complimented me, and I was like, oh, my God. He said something about how helpful I'd been, how he appreciates everything I've done for him, and it made me feel so good. I mean, I don't get that too often, so I was glad about that, but underneath, when I saw how my life must appear to someone else, it made me sad. It's sad to be this way. I don't have a life. That's the way I am. I don't have a life. I just pretty much go home, and that's it. Those guys at the video store? They know me. By four-thirty, if I haven't come in, they're sitting there waiting on me. They're like, 'Felecia, you're late.'"

Sometimes, Weston will be talking to a veteran seated across her desk, going over his file, when all of a sudden her arm will fall to her side and she'll go numb all over, a problem her doctors can't explain. Or, the headaches will overtake her and she'll need to excuse herself from the room. Or, her voice will start shaking and the poor guy with whom she's working won't be able to make out what she's trying to say. She rides out such moments because she knows they will soon pass, but she also knows that they will come again. Her therapist tells her she needs to work her way through these moments, to reach beyond the guilt she feels at having survived. By reaching, Weston hopes to pull her clients along with her. She throws herself into her work, determined that no other veteran will have to face what she is facing—or, at least, that no other veteran will have to face it alone.

THE FOUR S'S OF LIFE

Roberto Barrera
U.S. Marine Corps, Vietnam War

Roberto "Bobby" Barrera grew up in the kind of small Texas town that shows up in Larry McMurtry books—hardscrabble, God-fearing, strong-willed, enveloping. Folks left their front doors open, their keys in the ignition, and their hearts on their sleeves.

Del Rio, Texas, approximately one hundred fifty miles west of San Antonio and a good holler from the Rio Grande, is pretty much the same place today as it was when Barrera was a child during the 1950s. Then, his father was the police chief and his mother worked in a blue jean factory down the road. Now, nobody leaves their front doors unlocked anymore and the new pick-up trucks are all alarmed, but the essence of the community is much the same. Barrera isn't the only Del Rio native of his generation who's chosen to stay on. He's never lived anyplace else, aside from college and the military, and he doesn't care to move.

Del Rio suits him.

To the locals, it's hard to imagine a small town that's given more to her country than Del Rio has—certainly not one in recent memory. At one point, during the height of the Vietnam War, town leaders counted fourteen of their own among the nation's dead, and, after that, folks stopped counting. It was too depressing to have their shared suffering reduced to a statistic like that, too dispiriting, and so they looked instead to the number of young Del Rio men who made it back home. In that number, at least, there was something to celebrate. In that number, there was a kind of hope.

Bobby Barrera made it back, but just barely. He was riding with seven other Marines atop an armored personnel carrier when a command-detonated mine was set off directly beneath him. He lost his left arm and his right hand to a raging infection caused by the resulting burns—and most of his face was disfigured as well. Further, he lost much of the next few years to extensive surgeries, rehabilitation, and recovery. It was some time longer before he could reclaim the sense of place and purpose that now defines him—a sense he knew he would only find in Del Rio, if he could find it at all.

"There was nowhere else to go after that but home," he says. "Nowhere else I'd rather be."

Barrera was the fourth child in a family of five, and the first to go to college. It was a distinction he could have done without at the time. He'd wanted to go directly into the service following high school—the war in Southeast Asia was a powerful pull to a patriotic young man—but his father persuaded him to put it off until he finished college, so Barrera won an educational deferment and set about pursuing his father's dream. "It's funny," Barrera tells, "but he was the reason I wanted to join the military. That's where my dream came from. My father had served in World War Two, in Italy, and he used to tell us stories. He kept a picture of the Leaning Tower of Pisa, which I always thought was neat. I never knew anyone else who had been there. And he told me how, when he was in combat and there was artillery fire, he could actually hear the shell as it flew overhead if you listened for it. He'd tell me that and I would think, yeah, right. I didn't believe him. Of course, when I got to Vietnam and heard it for myself, I thought, okay, so that's what Dad was talking about."

His father had been in the army, but Barrera longed to be a marine; he used to swing by the recruiter's office in the federal building downtown and admire the Marine Corps uniform. They had the different recruiting posters on display for the different branches of service, and he imagined himself in that uniform. He's embarrassed to admit it, but that's what sold him on the marines: the uniform. The blue pants with the red stripe. Barrera thought that was pretty smart and stylish.

But the Marines would have to wait, smart uniform or no. To please his father, who dearly wanted one of his children to receive a college education, Barrera enrolled at a junior college in San Antonio, although he didn't exactly take to it in the ways his father had hoped. In fact, he didn't take to it much at all. "I passed a few classes," he says, with self-deprecating modesty. "I think the P.E. classes I did extremely well in, but mostly I partied. I spent my father's money. I drank his money. Didn't learn a whole bunch."

He did learn one important lesson, however. He learned to live his own life for himself, to pursue his own dreams and not a dream held by someone else on his behalf—even if that someone else was his own father. And so, after two misspent years in junior college, he was off to the Marine Corps recruiting depot in San Diego for basic training, and from there to infantry training at Camp Pendleton. He felt, for the first time, that his life was about to begin—and his first taste of battle wasn't far behind.

"We flew in to DaNang," he says, "and on our very first night in camp, one of the Vietcong infiltrated our perimeter. We lost one guy right then and there, and I thought to myself, what am I into?"

Luckily for Barrera, he had a platoon sergeant who took him under his wing and made it his special project to ease Barrera gently into the hard truths and horrors of the field. Unluckily, there wasn't much time for the new kid to learn the ropes. He arrived in country in August, 1969, and six weeks later—September 16, 1969—he was working out of a landing zone about fifty miles south of DaNang, preparing to cross a field in a convoy of personnel carriers. He'd been out on patrol for the previous ten days, and the night before, he'd managed a small celebration with some of the other Hispanic men in his platoon in honor of Mexico's Independence Day. Someone brought out some warm beer, and the guys drank it eagerly. There wasn't enough beer to go around, and there wasn't that much time to drink it anyway because they were making ready at first light, but Barrera guesses he remembers the small celebration because of what happened next.

The following morning, early, Barrera and company moved to a nearby field, where the convoy was being set up. His group was initially assigned to the first personnel carrier in the convoy—an unenviable position, he explains, "because if you hit a land mine, the first one's going to buy it." As it happened, he was later transferred to the third vehicle in the convoy. It was a welcome piece of good fortune to a guy like Barrera, who failed to account for the fact that he then would be traveling with the renowned marine sniper Carlos Hathcock. Gunnery Sergeant Hathcock was known for his extraordinary marksmanship and his fearless stalking of the Vietcong behind enemy lines. His ninety-three confirmed kills made him one of the icons of the Vietnam War, especially among his fellow marines; it also made him an attractive enemy target. It was widely known that there was a bounty on his head, a fact of the jungle that merely added to Hathcock's legend. To Barrera, at just that moment, Hathcock loomed as larger than life, and he recalls thinking it a great honor to ride with him and a marine intelligence officer, Lieutenant Ed Hyland, in the convoy. There was no room in his thinking for the prospect that this piece of good fortune would turn out to be a misfortune as well.

"We pulled out around nine o'clock," he explains, "and the first two carriers proceeded across that field without incident, and, in the back of the line, we all started to think we'd be okay."

But Charlie had only one target in mind on that morning—Sergeant Carlos Hathcock. He wore a trademark white feather in his jungle cap, and his fellow marines had made no real effort to conceal him from Vietcong who might have been tracking his movements. He traveled atop the carrier with everyone else, his signature feather visible to anyone in the surrounding jungle with a scope. As he crossed that field, he was a sitting duck, and Barrera was a sitting duck right alongside him.

"It was a remote-control, command-detonated mine," Barrera says. "They could have blown it up whenever they wanted to. Hathcock was the target. The rest of us were just along for the ride."

Barrera was thrown from the carrier in the explosion, along with the other seven men aboard. Several of the marines were severely burned. Barrera was knocked unconscious, but when he was roused by a medic from one of the other carriers in the convoy, he found that he could move about on his own. He was in pain, but he couldn't identify the source of the pain; he was alert, but he was, and remains, a little fuzzy on the details.

The supporting marines fired into the thick of surrounding jungle, and Hathcock, Barrera, and the other six wounded marines were ushered to the safety of a nearby chopper amidst an intense firefight. Barrera saw the chopper land and thought to himself, I need to get in that baby. All eight marines from that third carrier survived the explosion, and all eight, including Hathcock and Hyland, were able to walk onto that chopper, which took them to the USS *Repose*, a navy hospital ship back up the coast in DaNang. All eight stepped from the chopper onto waiting stretchers, and it was there, finally, that Barrera was first given any pain medications. He was confused, trying to get his mind around what had happened, trying to source the intense, all-over pain that seemed to hold him in a kind of tortuous vice. He'd suffered killing burns over most of his body, and he needed only to look across at some of the other guys to imagine what kind of shape he was in. Their skin, in places, was just peeling from their bodies around their faces, their arms, their torsos. It called to Barrera's feverish mind the way you'd peel off a latex dishwashing glove, the way the skin was just hanging.

He couldn't picture what he looked like himself, but he imagined the worst.

"They must have asked me my name twenty times," he says now, "and all kinds of other questions. Just to keep me talking, really. That's all I remember, really, from my time on the *Repose*. A whole lot of talking, which they told me later was to prevent shock from setting in."

Most of what Barrera knows of the following weeks came from what he was later told. He was so heavily and constantly sedated on the USS *Repose* that his memories are a blur. By the next afternoon, he was stable enough to be transferred off the ship to a hospital in Yokota, Japan, where he remained for another three days. The burns to Barrera's face and torso were so extensive that doctors worried about infection. In burn patients, Barrera was later told, there's a particular infection called phycomycosis that can spread through the body like gangrene if left unchecked. Back in 1969, there was no proven method of treatment for it other than to amputate the infected part of the body before the infection could spread. Now, more than thirty years later, there are antibiotics and other treatments available, even out in the field, but there was nothing in place that might have helped Barrera.

Still largely unaware of his precarious condition, Barrera was sent back to the United States to the burn center at Fort Sam Houston in San Antonio. When he stepped from the bus into the warm Texas air, he noticed a pick-up game of softball being played on the hospital grounds and thought to himself, gee, wouldn't it be nice to get a game in? He knew he'd suffered some serious burns and that he was facing potentially calamitous infections, but, at the same time, he felt energetic enough to imagine himself into a game of softball. It was, he says now, a curious thing, to be facing such dire circumstances and, at the same time, be able-bodied enough to regret that he wasn't out there playing ball. He'd been a ballplayer in high school, and even the force of that landmine could not obliterate that part of him.

As Barrera recalls, all eight marines injured in that convoy were sent to the same burn center. None stayed as long as Barrera did. And none were surrounded by the warm embrace of friends and family like he was. Del Rio, Texas, was less than a three-hour drive from San Antonio, so the burn center was teaming with Barreras. There was a sister who lived in town and a girlfriend who came almost every day. And the rest of Barrera's big family regularly made the trip to be by his bedside. His parents all but pulled up a chair and moved in. Barrera had only been gone for six weeks, and they were grateful that he wasn't one of those dispiriting Del Rio statistics, that he had made it home alive.

Barrera remained heavily sedated. He was wheeled in and out of surgery so often that he has no clear memory of those first weeks, as army doctors struggled to avoid excessive amputations. The burns and the skin grafts were bad enough, the agonizing bath treatments worse still, but the phycomycosis fungus had taken hold and moved swiftly and painlessly through Barrera's upper body. Surgeons cut off his left arm at the elbow, thinking that they could stop the infection, but a subsequent biopsy showed that it had run to his bicep, so they did a second amputation—a disarticulation—to where his left shoulder used to be.

"I didn't really know why they were amputating," recalls Barrera, who also lost his right hand to the resulting infection. "I'll never forget the look on this one doctor's face. He came in to tell me they were going to take three fingers off my hand because of the fungus, just three fingers, and he was real apologetic about it. Like maybe I'd think it was his fault. And I thought to myself, well, three fingers. That wasn't too bad. Three fingers. I guessed I could live like that. But then I woke up after the surgeries and the entire hand was gone. I never knew how serious the situation was, and they never really told me."

Barrera remained on the burn unit for three months in intensive care. He was in and out of that hospital for the next three years, and had thirty-two separate surgeries, eventually including extensive plastic surgery to his face. His entire lip had to be removed, and his ears had been infected as well, and, beyond that, the skin needed to be replaced over 20 percent of his body.

For the longest time, Barrera lay in his hospital bed in a deep depression. He couldn't face what his future might be without his arms. Hell, he couldn't even face himself in the mirror. Every day, he was made to endure a series of horribly excruciating baths, a course of treatment that went on for months, until his burns healed, and he found himself thinking he didn't want to live like this. He didn't think he had it in him to tough it out. All along, he'd told himself that as long as he could keep his legs, he'd be okay. That was the bargain he'd made with himself—sometimes, even, in prayer—and he was not sure he could keep up his end. He couldn't see a lifetime without a leg. He figured he could find a way to cope with whatever else came his way, but a couple of weeks after he lost his second arm, he began to lose his will to live. What had once been a kind of fire in his belly had been all but smothered by the pain and by the uncertainties ahead.

"I was feeling down," he says now. "I didn't want to go on. I didn't see the point. And then, my father came in to see me on the intensive care unit. I wasn't really thinking, but I saw him and started to think, hey, this is my ticket out of this misery. He wasn't in uniform, but I knew he had a gun. He always carried a gun, on or off duty. You're the chief of police, you carry a gun. So he reached over to my bed, and I said to him, 'Dad, do you have your gun?' I knew the answer, but I asked anyway. And he said, 'Yes, why?' I don't think he had any idea where I was going with this, and, to tell the truth, I didn't have any real idea where I was going with this. I didn't. It was just coming out of me. And I told him I wanted him to shoot me, put me out of my misery. What a thing for a son to have to ask his father, and I hated that I was asking him, but I couldn't see another way. I'd have done it myself, but my hands were gone, and I couldn't figure how to pull the trigger. I told him I didn't think I could live like this. He sat with me for the longest time, and we cried together, and he talked me down from whatever I was feeling."

That wasn't the first time Barrera felt suicidal, but it was the first time he moved to act on those feelings, the first time he gave them voice. And it wasn't the last time, either, only from then on, he had his father's strength and he added it to his own in what ways he could. The fire inside had been rekindled, or at least been given a breath of air.

Barrera was sent home in time for Christmas (he went back to the hospital after the holidays for another three-month stretch), but he didn't think he was ready. Physically, it was probably a good thing for him to get out and moving again, but emotionally, it may have been too soon. He didn't want anyone to see him. It was bad enough that his parents had to see him like that, and the rest of his family, and his girlfriend, but the thought of his buddies back in Del Rio coming by for a visit . . . well, that was too much. He didn't know that he would ever be ready for that, but he certainly wasn't ready just yet. Doctors had yet to begin the extensive reconstructive and plastic surgeries to his face. His entire upper lip was gone. He was all gums and teeth, from the bottom of his nose to the sides of his mouth. His left arm was gone, too, and he'd only recently begun to work with the prosthetic hook they'd given him to take the place of his right hand.

"I told my parents I didn't want any visitors," he says. "I had three close buddies, and I knew they'd come by, but I was very clear about it. I didn't want to see them. Sure enough, they came over the evening I arrived home. They would not be turned away. They knew better than I did what was best for me. I'm sure they were shocked to see me like that, but nobody said anything. They didn't show it, either. They just started kidding around, same as they'd always done. Someone suggested we go out and get a beer, but I wasn't comfortable with that, so we decided to go down to a little convenience store about six blocks from the house. They dragged me along. I got in the back seat, and when we got to the store, I couldn't open the door. I don't think I was wearing my hook, but anyway, I just couldn't open the door. The other three, they'd all gotten out of the car and were waiting for me in the parking lot. They'd kind of just forgotten about me, and then it dawned on them that I was still in the car. And they all started laughing. It was the funniest thing. I laughed, too. They were like, oh, shit, we forgot about you. Things were back to the way they were, before all this shit happened, just like that."

It was one thing to be accepted by his friends and family, and quite another to move about in the rest of the world. He still couldn't look at himself in the mirror, so how the hell did he expect anyone else to look at him? Barrera's depression ran deeper than vanity, however. He soon drifted apart from the girlfriend who had been by his side during his first months home, and, before he knew it, she was engaged to someone else. He felt rootless and alone. He couldn't think how to jumpstart the rest of his life, what to do with his days. Nothing interested him or motivated him. He thought about finishing school, but he couldn't imagine how to go about it. Without his hands, how would he take notes, or sit for exams, or write term papers? It was easier not to bother than to try and fail. With that complacency, there was no good reason for Barrera to leave his parents' house each day, except to go to the convenience store for another couple of six packs.

He went on in this way for months—years, even — shuttling back and forth to San Antonio for another surgery or treatment, living with his parents, drinking beer, struggling to string enough days together to call it a week. "I had no direction," he says, "no goals. It was just one day to the next. Drinking beer and stumbling in at two and three in the morning. My parents weren't about to say anything, but my act was wearing thin."

The turning point came when he met his future wife, Maricelia. One of Barrera's buddies was actually dating her sister, and he kept trying to set him up with another of her sisters. (She came from a big family.) But Barrera had his heart set on Maricelia. He kept saying, "No, I like that one," and he went calling on a regular basis. It turned out they'd known each other, but only in passing. She wasn't put off by his appearance or his apparent lack of direction. She saw Barrera

for the person he might become, and when they were
married six months later—in April, 1974—she set
about whipping him into shape. She knew what was
best for him, he says now. She knew what he meant
when he couldn't think how to put it. She heard the
truth between the lines of his bullshit.

Soon, Barrera's world came into focus. He decided
that he wanted to be a counselor, to help others through
the difficult paces he had barely managed for himself.
He finished college and started working toward his master's degree. He and Maricelia adopted three children:
Rene, Aldo, and Karla. He took a job teaching psychol-
ogy, English, and Spanish at his old high school in Del
Rio. Five years later, master's in hand, he became a
counselor for the juvenile department in town; five years
after that, he moved on to another counseling position.
"I was hooked on these five-year plans," he reflects.
"Then it was, okay, let's find something else to do."

Finally, after the relatively short-term stops and
starts, he landed in his present position, as director of
the Family Support Center at the Laughlin Air Force
Base, supervising and conducting various counseling
programs for servicemen and their families, and he's
not going anyplace anytime soon. He guesses that the
main reason he's lasted at the job beyond his customary
five years is because each day is different, and there
have been endless opportunities to create new programs
and adopt new initiatives. He and his staff of ten provide parenting classes, financial planning classes, support groups, employment counseling—everything a
family might need when a spouse is sent overseas.

Every year, when September 16 rolls around on the calendar, Barrera pauses in his busy day to reflect on the blast that redirected his life. Typically, he's at work. He closes the door and, for a few minutes, some time around nine o'clock, he sits and wonders at the twists and turns his life has taken, at the positive difference he's managed to make in the lives of his clients, at the guiding hands he and Maricelia have extended to their three children, at the role model he has become despite himself. He considers his dwindling list of regrets—that he has never held his wife's hand or played catch with his children in the backyard—and weighs them against his triumphs and figures he's come out ahead.

Along the way, Barrera became a powerful motivational speaker, a role he never would have imagined for himself when he was struggling with his appearance and his uncertain future all those years ago. He put together a presentation he has now given to hundreds of schools, churches, and community and leadership groups around the country on what Barrera calls "the four S's of life": support, sense of humor, a spiritual relationship, and a strong sense of self. Each S, he says, is like an essential building block, upon which we stand to reach our goals; lose a single one, and we might never reach as high as we would on all four. He might have been a little bit slow in identifying these aspects of his own life, but once he did, the foundation was strong.

"I had a tremendous amount of support," he says. Indeed, his father took off nearly two months of work to remain by his side at Fort Sam Houston, and his mother didn't miss a day. A crowd of friends and family filled the waiting area outside Barrera's room on the ICU burn unit, uncertain if he'd survive, but knowing that if he did, they would be there for him, each one of them, in what ways they could. The support continued into his rehabilitation and recovery, from his wife ("She became my other hand," he says), and an army therapist, Captain Starla Swerda, who shared with Barrera words of wisdom that have resonated every day since. "She taught me that people were going to stare at me for the rest of my life," he reflects, "and that I had better get used to it or stay home and go down the drain."

As for a sense of humor . . . well, Barrera had always had a good one and needed merely to rediscover it for himself. "As down as I was, I always managed to laugh," he says. One time, he teamed up with a friend he made on the burn unit, a guy who'd lost his legs to a similar infection, because both of them were pining one hot afternoon for a Coke from the soda machine down the hall. "He had no legs, so he couldn't get down there himself," Barrera says. "And I had no arms, so I couldn't get the coins in the slots, so we improvised. I told him to get on my back, and we'd make a go of it together, and that's what we did. He was a big guy, but we managed. Made quite a picture, I imagine, the two of us, doing what we could to get down to that soda machine. I'll tell you what, though. That was the best darn Coke I've ever had."

There were also many and varied ways he caught folks by surprise—most especially, his Aunt Ida—with the three sets of prosthetic ears he was issued at the hospital. "It's amazing how much fun you can have with three sets of ears," he says mischievously.

"You have to laugh," he insists. "You just do. It's a part of life. And it's not just that you have to laugh at yourself, but you have to laugh along with everyone else. Some things are just too funny. Life is just too funny. And kids, they'll get you every time. I've got kids coming up to me every day, asking questions that seem to embarrass their parents, but I don't mind them at all. Actually, I enjoy it." One of his all-time favorites: "How do you wipe your butt, Mister?"

Spirituality has always played an important part in Barrera's life, dating back to childhood, but it's taken on a more featured role since his injuries. Still, he's careful to emphasize in his talks that the relevant concept of spirituality does not necessarily carry a devoutly religious component. You need to have a sense that the world is bigger than just you, he says, a sense that we are all held accountable to each other, that there's a reason we're here on this Earth other than to satisfy our own impulses. In his own case, Barrera looks back on September 16, 1969, as the day his life took shape. It is ironic, he knows, that the events that left him misshapen have, over time, given shape and focus to his days, but he figures God had a plan for him, all along.

"I have a purpose in life," he says, "and that's been to help other military families through some of what I had to go through. If I had to go through it myself in order to help others, I'm okay with that. Do I wish it hadn't happened? Absolutely. I wish I could change it, but I can't, so I'm comfortable to the extent that something positive could come out of it. It's all part of the journey God has in mind for me."

And finally, he concludes in his presentation, you need to have a strong sense of self. "You need to be able to look at yourself in the mirror and say, 'I am the most important person in my life,'" he maintains. Here he points to his own name for emphasis: *Barrera*, Spanish for obstacle, or barrier, or challenge. "I was my own obstacle to getting on with my life because I couldn't get past what had happened and move on to what might happen next."

Barrera closes his talks in answer to the child who innocently offered up that all-time favorite question, reinforcing the self-deprecating sense of humor and abundant good cheer that have resonated with audiences all over the country. "Very carefully," he says.

I'm Not Done

Michael McElhiney
U.S. Army Special Forces Team, Afghanistan War

It takes a special breed of soldier to seek Special Forces training, and of those special few, only a small percentage make the cut. There's an arduous selection process and a series of Q—or, qualifying—courses that can stretch over several years, covering field and weapons training, patrolling tactics, foreign language proficiency, commission of warfare training, and survival and evasion training. Beyond these quantifiable measures, there's also a certain special something required of Special Forces candidates, something that's hard to identify, harder still to teach, and impossible to ignore.

Either you've got it or you don't, and if you've got it, you're intensively trained to do whatever it takes to overcome whatever obstacle you might face—against every imaginable enemy, against every unimaginable condition.

"It's a different army," reports Sergeant 1st Class Michael McElhiney of the Army's 3rd Battalion 5th Special Forces Group, also known as the Green Berets.

"You always see these guys, and you hear about these guys, and they're pretty impressive when you're a young soldier. You look up to them and think, wow, and you look at the movies, John Wayne and Rambo, and think, look at those guys. And after a while, it comes to you that if you're going to make a career in the military, you might as well be the best."

McElhiney and his fellow Green Berets worked valiantly during Operation Enduring Freedom to rescue Afghan citizens who had helped resist the oppressive Taliban regime. McElhiney's team was traveling with Hamid Karzai, Afghanistan's interim prime minister and an ever-growing coalition of Afghan and U.S. soldiers—an oddly rag-tag band of the army's elite and a loosely assembled supporting force—when they were struck by friendly fire on a hill approximately eighteen kilometers north of Kandahar. Twenty-seven people were killed: three American soldiers and twenty-four Afghan coalition fighters. Forty more were wounded, including Karzai, who suffered superficial glass and shrapnel cuts to the face, and McElhiney. McElhiney had been standing approximately forty meters from the top of a hill, where a two thousand-pound bomb was mistakenly dropped from an American B-52 fighter plane. McElhiney lost his right arm in the blast and suffered a collapsed lung.

Six weeks later, as the nation saluted, he was seated in Washington, D.C., two seats from First Lady Laura Bush during President George W. Bush's State of the Union address.

"It all happened so fast," recalls McElhiney, whose strapping, movie-star looks cast him as a photo opportunity waiting to happen—as, indeed, it frequently has ever since President Bush called public attention to his heroism. "The blast, the triage, the amputation. Next thing I know, I'm touring the Pentagon, meeting some of our congressmen and senators. I was still on a lot of medication, still recuperating, but there was this whole day of activities. And to be singled out like that, with two other members of our team, it was an incredible honor."

For a young man with a proud family history of military service and a hard-charging, quietly heroic dignity, it was an honor that resonated over several generations, over centuries, even. At one point, McElhiney's grandmother researched the family tree and determined that at least one family member had served in every American war since the Revolutionary War. His family fairly pulsed with a call to service—his father had served in Vietnam with the United States Navy—so it's no wonder McElhiney was drawn to it as well. As a high school student in Kansas City, Missouri, college didn't hold any real appeal, so he considered his options. "Basically, it came down to which branch of the service I would join," he recalls. His sister had joined the navy, but McElhiney decided to join the army. It wasn't that he was contrary; he saw himself as more of a soldier, and yet as he moved through the ranks, he found himself stationed in Germany, in the mechanized infantry, overseeing vehicle maintenance of the motor pool. It was there that he started to think about Special Forces.

"I was kinda stuck," he says. "I didn't really like what I was doing, I wasn't too happy, and the more I looked into it, Special Forces seemed to be the next logical step."

By this time, McElhiney was married, with two young children, Michael and Maria. His wife Judy was also in the military. His future was comfortable and certain, but he looked up from his work one day and realized the army he knew was not the army he joined. He wasn't happy, or challenged, or excited. He wanted to feel like he was making a difference, like he mattered, and it was hard to feel that way in the motor pool. He was twenty-three years old, looking to make a career in the service, and he was bored.

"There's actually a long period in there, from when you put in for Special Forces to when you actually get to the selection process," he says. "That whole time, I was just raring to go. I was waiting to hear, and waiting to hear, but in my head I was gone."

Gone, eventually, to Fort Bragg, Kentucky, where McElhiney embarked on a weeks-long testing and selection phase designed, he guesses, to thin the herd of applicants to a manageable number. "They put you through every kind of test," he says. "Classroom tests, humanities and geography, that sort of thing, to tests of physical endurance, long runs, pushing vehicles, sleep deprivation, everything you can think of. There's this one test, you gather in an open area with, say, six six-foot ropes, twelve ten-foot poles, and a couple fifty-five gallon drums, and you're given orders to move this and that from here to there. 'You've got this much time. Do you have any questions? Go!' It's just days and days of that, and it wears on you after a while, and people get hurt, or they drop out, or they decide it's not what they want to do after all, or the Special Forces guys decide you're not what they were looking for."

McElhiney estimates that there were more than three hundred soldiers invited into the selection process with him, and less than one hundred graduated to the Q course phase, where the applicant pool was trimmed even further.

"Once I made the decision to stay in the military, and make a career in the military, I wanted to be on top," he says of his determination to reach the other end of the selection process. "Or, at least, where I perceived to be the top. The Green Berets, that was it for me, the best of the best. There's a lot of little things I was doing, early on in my career, didn't seem to matter all that much. We'd do stuff for no reason. If a jeep broke down, we'd repair it or replace it. If you fell asleep on guard duty, what was the big deal? No lives were at stake. Our freedom wasn't at stake. It didn't really matter. I wanted to be where there were consequences."

Five active duty groups comprise the army's Special Operations Forces team, along with two reserve groups. Three battalions per group, three line companies per battalion, five teams per company. McElhiney was assigned to the Fifth Special Forces Group in August, 1996—the legendary Green Berets outfit that had come to prominent, hard-charging attention during the Vietnam War. He had been raring to go for so long that any assignment would have been welcome, but the Fifth Group, to McElhiney, was extra special; it came with a reputation, and a charge to uphold it.

The Middle East was the basic area of operation for the Fifth Group, which used Fort Campbell, Kentucky, as a base of operations, although the group had just returned from a mission in Haiti when McElhiney joined up with them. He remembers it being like night and day, the contrast between the mechanized infantry and what he was soon being asked to do. He also remembers feeling frustrated, somewhat, at missing out on the operation in Haiti. It was all the other guys were talking about. After all that time, waiting to be let in, looking to make a difference, he felt he might never see any real action. Still, he was on the move constantly, mountain climbing, sky diving, scuba diving. He was having the time of his life, traveling the world, training to make a difference, pushing the envelope of human experience. He had wanted to be where there were consequences, and he was making ready.

On September 11, 2001, McElhiney was in Kazakhstan on a scheduled training maneuver when word reached his group that the Pentagon and the World Trade Center towers had been attacked. Over the next hours, as Al Qaeda and Osama bin Laden and the Taliban became household names throughout the United States, McElhiney thought his group might be deployed directly to Afghanistan, where bin Laden was thought to be headquartered and where al-Qaeda training camps dotted the countryside. He and his colleagues worried that some of their mission-critical equipment wouldn't make it through unless they could pack it and prepare it themselves, but they awaited their orders. They would go where they were needed, with whatever equipment they could get their hands on.

Apparently, the army brass had some of these same worries because the Green Berets were sent back to Fort Campbell by the end of that first week and told to await word on their deployment. They were going to Afghanistan, but they weren't going just yet.

"We went immediately into isolation," McElhiney says, which essentially meant there was to be no contact with anyone outside Fifth Group, including spouses and immediate family members. While awaiting a specific assignment, the team conducted an exhaustive area study and made general plans. There was a good deal of military intelligence from 1980, when the Russians had invaded Afghanistan, and McElhiney's team spent the time being briefed and prepped. They learned the land and the language, the history and the people. They learned about terror networks and cells. They talked through their mission from every conceivable angle—and from some inconceivable ones, as well. Whatever intelligence there was on the region, these men made it their own as they waited for their orders to come through. There was no communication with family members—or anyone else outside the group— but as they waited on word, McElhiney thought back to his father's tour in Vietnam, which had become an unpopular war at home by the time his father returned. Here, McElhiney was preparing to fight with an almost unwavering show of public support, and the contrast was galvanizing.

"We were all so angry," he says. "We watched that second plane hit the tower and there was this surge of patriotism, this wave of rising up and protecting our freedom, and as it happened, we were in a position to do something about it. We had a place to put that anger, but it was more than that. It was all those skills we'd spent all that time developing. All those techniques. All that Special Forces training. It would be an unconventional war, and that's what Green Berets do. That's our bread and butter. And the American people were behind us all the way."

Still, McElhiney reports that there was some apprehension among his group as well. They were facing an unknowable enemy. They had all this time to think about it, all this talk of caves and underground terror networks, and their minds had a chance to run away from them. They worried about their families. They took in non-military reports on the Taliban and the al-Qaeda terror network, documentaries on public television and the Discovery channel, and started to think these guys were the baddest thing around. They were thinking things to death, itching to get over there and on the ground and down to business. A lot of the men had never seen real combat before, so there was that worry too.

For a unit built on contingency training and meticulous detail, an unconventional war against an unknowable enemy can be a worrisome thing, especially if you have too much time to worry. September rolled into October, and Fifth Group still hadn't been deployed. All they knew was that they were going, and soon, only soon couldn't happen quickly enough for McElhiney.

"By the time we got over there, in early November, all of that theory and doctrine was pretty much out the window," he says. "We'd thought through every eventuality but the ones we actually found. About the only certainty was that we were to link up with Hamid Karzai somewhere in southern Afghanistan. We didn't know how we were going in. We didn't know when we were going. We just knew were going."

Karzai was an influential political figure in Afghanistan who would play a significant role in the U.S. operation there. His father had been executed for speaking out against the Taliban and al-Qaeda, and he had been living in exile in Pakistan up until the attack on the World Trade Center and the Pentagon. Throughout his exile, Karzai maintained important relationships with tribal chiefs and village leaders in the southern part of the country, and the Special Forces mission was to harness that support into a fighting force of Afghan soldiers.

"We were promised a force of five hundred men," McElhiney says, "but like everything else in an unconventional war, nothing is as you expect it to be. In fact, everything is pretty much the opposite of what these people tell you. If they tell you next week, it's next month. If they tell you a guy is six feet tall, he's two feet tall. If they tell you to expect five hundred soldiers, you'll end up with thirty. And that's basically what we found when we got over there. There was no real force to speak of, not in the beginning. A few guys who wanted to fight with us, but nothing had been set up in any kind of organized way. We had to collect Afghan soldiers as we moved through each region. We would supply them with guns and ammunition and equipment. We would train them. We would pay them. And eventually we assembled a sizeable force, and add to our ranks as we moved down towards Kandahar, but in the beginning, we'd come through a village and see all these people wander out, and we'd have to look at each one and think, okay, he's a fighter. He's one of ours."

In one village, McElhiney and company helped an Afghan farmer track down a goat that had gotten loose from its pen, and, in gratitude, the farmer agreed to join the fight. In the north, Taliban fighters switched over to the Northern Alliance for similarly benign reasons or for no reason at all. (A day or two later, as circumstances changed, many switched sides again.) McElhiney figures the changes in allegiance had more to do with who had the biggest guns or the best prospects than with any shift in ideology or world view, but the net effect on Fifth Group was to leave the Americans leery of their presumed allies.

"You're not only watching out for the bad guys," McElhiney says, "but you're watching the guys around you. We were skeptical of almost everyone we had fighting with us because, really, they could turn on you any second. These guys would look at you and think, hey, that's a nice knife you've got there. Or, hey I could use a rifle like that. We knew that if we went down, they'd be going through our pockets before we hit the ground."

It was alongside this hastily assembled and dubiously qualified fighting force that Fifth Group swept across southern Pakistan, with interim Prime Minister Karzai rallying his countrymen along the way. "He really had a lot of influence with his people," McElhiney says. "He was educated. His father had played an important role during the Russian occupation. They listened to him the way someone in Boston would probably listen to a Kennedy. He genuinely seemed to care about the Afghan people. We would advise him militarily, and he would advise us politically. He was constantly on the phone with his people with the Northern Alliance. He kept a constant watch on the big picture. He knew what we needed to do."

By early December, 2001, McElhiney had been in isolation for nearly three months, which meant he had had no contact with his wife and family for that entire time. Letters from home were finally reaching him in the field, but he was unable to write in return.

"I tried to put that part of it out of my mind," he says. "We had said our goodbyes. We had written our 'death letters' and handed them in to the chaplain. We had talked several times about getting killed. We were prepared for it. We talked about it with each other, and we'd talked about it with our wives and families before signing on. It was part of the deal. We didn't know what we were facing. We didn't know what our outcome was going to be. The only piece in our control was to do our job and do it bravely. If we're going to go, we're going to go. The only thing that was certain was that we wouldn't get captured. That was the one absolute. There was a price on our heads the day we set down. There was a price just on our uniforms. So that was a given: we would not be captured. But we weren't going to wimp out. We had our jobs to do. We had to lead these people. And that was the thing about the Afghan people, they wanted us to lead them. They needed us to lead them. If we went ten steps forward, they'd go ten steps forward. If we went ten forward and one back, they'd go ten forward and one back. They followed our lead in everything we did, and if they saw us backing down, that would have been the end."

On December 3, 2001, the Green Berets and Afghan coalition fighters looked to occupy a small town approximately two kilometers west of a bridge that stood as the last key terrain feature en route to Kandahar. Their objective was to take the town and then to take the bridge, and, from there, begin the push down to the city. McElhiney was part of a split team, the forward deployed element; Karzai was held back with the rear unit, on the theory that if the advance engagement did not go well, the lead team would take the hit and Karzai would be spared. He was too valuable to put at unnecessary risk.

McElhiney says that his group met minimal resistance in the town and suffered no casualties, and when the firefight was over, the townspeople spilled from their homes and thanked the Americans for liberating them. It had been that way on the entire push south toward Kandahar. The Afghan coalition fighters would pause to pray before moving in, a brief firefight would ensue, and Afghan villagers would spill from their homes in gratitude.

By the time the small town was secure, it was nearly nightfall. The Special Forces team determined that they would not take the bridge until the next morning. However, several of the Afghan fighters, overjoyed at this latest victory and unfamiliar with the concept of orders and a chain of command, went down to the bridge on their own, and continued their celebration there. At approximately ten-thirty that evening, the Taliban launched an aggressive counterattack across that bridge, killing dozens of the allied Afghan fighters and clearing a path back to the small town the Special Forces Group had only recently secured. A day of intense fighting followed, ranging from close, small-arms battles to aggressive air support. After all that training, all those months studying tactics and weapons, McElhiney and his fellow Green Berets were finally put to the test, and McElhiney recalls feeling primed and poised and pumped.

"Whatever they threw at us, we were ready," he says.

The Special Forces team did take one serious hit—a sniper shot to the neck of a soldier named Wes McGear, and as his buddies moved him to the Medivac, the Afghans tried to move with them. "We were like, no, no, no," McElhiney says. "We were telling them to stay put, we'd be right back, but they were like, no, no, no. If you go, we go. There was a whole lot of confusion."

Eventually, the U.S. coalition established a base on a small hill overlooking the entire area—the only vantage point that offered an unobstructed view of the entire area—and settled in for the night. The bridge was lost, but they would make another push for it in the morning. The hilltop was level, about the size of the foundation of a single-family home. The men called it the Alamo.

"We should have never called it the Alamo," McElhiney says.

Late that night, a headquarters element joined the coalition atop the hill, bringing fourteen additional Special Forces soldiers, some new trucks, and a U.S. mailbag. There were letters and boxes from home. McElhiney got a windfall: six boxes of food and assorted goodies, and six letters. There was a canned ham, candy, vitamins, cookies, magazines. He distributed a good deal of the food to the Afghan fighters, specifically to the twenty or so men who had become part of an informal security platoon. "By this time, we had a pool of Afghan fighters we semi-trusted," McElhiney says, "and there was one guy in charge of this group who we called the Sergeant Major. The Afghan SarMajor. We'd call for him, and he'd come running."

At daylight, McElhiney was down from the top of the hill, loading some of the new trucks with five-gallon cans of gasoline, when all of a sudden he saw a big red flash, which was quickly followed by an enormous explosion. It was like the inside of a thunderclap, a burst of light and sound that caught everyone on that hill completely and terrifyingly by surprise. The next thing McElhiney knew, he was facing downhill, his right thumb almost touching the crease of his right elbow in a position that was more painful to look at than to experience. McElhiney thought to himself, okay, compound fracture. That was his training kicking in, his practiced composure. Assess the damage and deal with it. Pick yourself up and move on. But he couldn't pick himself up, or it didn't occur to him to attempt to do so, at least not right away. But he noticed all that gasoline leaking from the busted-up cans he'd been loading on to the truck, spilling onto the hard earth down to where he had fallen. Then he saw his right arm pointing down toward the ground in a way that had nothing to do with the rest of his position. Another compound fracture. He thought to himself, oh, that's bad. Finally, he tried to lift himself up and noticed a deep, sucking chest wound. He was gushing blood, and his blood had mixed with the gasoline to make it look a lot worse than it actually was. A deep, black-red spot about the size of a throw rug had formed at his side. He thought he'd been blown in half. His torso, he realized, felt unbearably hot. And then he blacked out.

What had happened, as near as anyone could figure, was the kind of equipment or communications failure that soldiers dread and commanders lose sleep over. Inexplicably, an American B-52 had dropped a two-thousand-pound bomb directly on the Fifth Group position atop the Alamo. Either someone gave or entered the wrong coordinates, or there was a colossal misfire, or the Taliban had orchestrated a masterful piece of sabotage. An official investigation was launched, but no results had been released at the time of this writing. The blast killed twenty-four Afghan fighters and three Americans. Scores were injured. Interim prime minister Karzai, who was inside a small building about one hundred meters from the blast, was severely cut around his face from flying shrapnel and broken glass, leaving him bloodied but strong enough to attend to others who had been more severely wounded. Others in the same building were killed instantly.

McElhiney didn't know it at the time, but there was a critically long wait for the wounded to be air-lifted to where they could receive proper medical attention. The nearest base was a marine camp with a remote desert airstrip, and it was a one-hour chop-per ride from the obliterated hill. In daylight, the MH-53 Pave Low helicopters were easy targets for Taliban fighters. And so, the marines took some extra precautions before taking off. Meanwhile, the Air Force Special Operations Wing base in Pakistan heard the same call and immediately dispatched two choppers to the scene. They didn't give a thought to the dangerous flying conditions; some of their own were down, and they would make it through, no mat-ter what.

McElhiney's captain, Jason Amerine, tried to keep his men comfortable while waiting for the choppers to arrive, but McElhiney was beyond comforting. He managed a small smile when Amerine told him he looked like hell, but he was in shock, drifting in and out of consciousness. The wound to his chest made it diffi-cult to breathe, and his cohorts looked at the tangle of his arm and the gaping wound to his chest and worried if he'd make it.

"One of the medics told me later that I actually crossed my legs while I was waiting for the choppers," he says. "Apparently, I kept talking, on and off, the entire time. I asked this medic for a glass of water, and when he returned with it, he told me he'd gotten me stable, that I was gonna be okay. I don't know, I guess that made me relax a bit because he says I crossed my legs at that point like I was kicking back. Did I? I suppose I could have. I had so much morphine in me at the time. One of the other guys said I was joking, so who knows?"

Four days later, McElhiney woke up on an ICU unit in a German hospital. He had undergone several surgeries, including the amputation of his right arm just below the elbow. There was no saving it, he was told. Hell, there was hardly anything even holding it to the rest of his body: one vein, one shred of muscle, one nerve, and one tendon. His wife and mother flew over to be with him, but he has no clear memory of the reunion. His captain came by to brief McElhiney on what had happened, although it was a few days more before McElhiney was able to process that he had been hit by friendly fire. It wouldn't register, not at first. Such a thing was so far removed from his thinking that he had a tough time getting his mind around it, especially through the cloud of pain medication in his system.

Now, with perspective, he shrugs off the circumstances of his injury. "It's not like it's gonna bring my arm back," he says, "whatever they find in their investigation. I think we've all got a good idea what happened, and I think it's important for the families who lost their sons and husbands and fathers to know for certain what happened, but for me, personally, I don't think it will change anything. It won't change the fact that we did good, important work in the weeks leading up to that explosion. It was a successful mission, all around. I would do it again, knowing the outcome. I'm proud of what we did. I mean, we had a pretty unique mission. We were some of the first ones in. Hamid Karzai is the leader of Afghanistan now, and he was our guy. We played a pretty big role in a pretty big world event. We made a little history."

McElhiney recuperated at Walter Reed Army Hospital in Washington, D.C., where he was fitted for his first prosthetic. As soon as he was well enough to travel, he returned to Fort Campbell, where he was given a Purple Heart and a Bronze Star, along with the other members of his Green Beret team. He also returned home to Kansas City, where he received a hero's welcome, and then back to Washington for the State of the Union address. And yet for all the pomp and ceremony, McElhiney reports that he was most interested in reuniting with Hamid Karzai, who was also in attendance for the president's address. After a brief photo opportunity and media session with the president and first lady, McElhiney and fellow Green Beret Ronnie Rakes sought Karzai out across the room. The three men talked about their shared mission. They talked about what their efforts meant to the Afghan people, what they meant in the global war against terrorism. They talked about the future. And, unavoidably, they talked about the friendly fire that kept them from that final push down to Kandahar and that took the lives of so many of their friends and allies.

"Yeah, it pissed me off," McElhiney says, "I won't lie about it. I had about eight days in there where I felt sorry for myself, and the good thing was, they weren't eight consecutive days. It just kinda hit me from time to time, but that's behind me now. This is my job, Special Forces, and this is what can happen. You don't mean for it to happen, but it happens. There are a lot of other ways I could have gotten hurt. I could have jumped out of a plane and have my parachute fail. I could have stepped on a mine. The point is, what's the difference if it was one of our weapons or one of theirs? I wasn't out there just because I got to wear a cool beret and because people thought I was some kind of mean, trained killer. No. You've got to do it all the way, play every scenario out in your head, the good and the bad. You don't become a professional football player just to drive a nice car and live in a nice house. You play because you love to play, and you accept the risks associated with playing. That's how I looked at my time in the field. I loved every minute of what I was doing, and I can't trade those minutes because of what happened."

No, but McElhiney can trade on his experience and continue to make a vital contribution to the Special Forces. He means to make a difference, still, and he means to serve the balance of his twenty years with distinction. "Last thing I wanted," he says, "and the thing I feared most, was to end up like some of those vets you see on the street. I thought the army would throw me out. I thought I'd be in and out of the VA, living on the street, begging for change. I've still got a lot to offer, so I'm not gonna start sniveling now and think, well, my arm's gone, I did my time, I'm done. I'm not done. I'm a long way from done. When I was sworn in, I didn't pledge to uphold our freedoms and make all these sacrifices until I got hurt or sick or until I had a bad day. That disgusts me, when people check out first chance they get. Not the guys I work with in Special Forces, but you see it all the time, all over the military, and that's just not me.

"First time I looked down at my prosthetic arm I cried. I was like, God, this is what I've got for the rest of my life. But with time, I realized I didn't have it so bad. I can do pretty much everything I could do before. I've taught myself to write with my left hand and to throw a ball. I can do push-ups. I can run and fire a weapon. I still play basketball and go mountain climbing and rock climbing. I can pass all of my physical tests. About the only thing I can't do is climb a rope and do pull-ups. I see these guys out at the winter sports clinic in Aspen, and they're blind or missing a leg or more than one limb, and they're still doing all these activities, activities that I hold dear, and I think to myself, I'm only missing a little part of my arm. This is nothing."

McElhiney doesn't expect to see any more time in the field, but he means to continue to make a difference in Special Forces as a day-to-day operations technician, as an instructor, as a role model to some of the new recruits, and to young people who express an interest in his story.

"I feel a little ripped off now," he says, "because all that good experience we gained in Afghanistan I could have put to good use in Iraq, but there are still things I can do, still things I can contribute. I can't be on the team anymore, I know that, but we need a lot of support people at the base or in the field, so I've got no idea what the next few years will bring. But like I said, I'm not done."

A CALL TO HELP

Charles A. Thompson Jr.
U.S. Marine Corps, Vietnam War

Charlie Thompson is one of those rare individuals who heard the call of duty twice, and the fact that he came back healthy after his first tour and somewhat less so after his second never left him regretting his decision to serve that second time.

Thompson grew up in Huntington, West Virginia, with adventure in his blood. His father was a West Point graduate who went on to a distinguished career with United Airlines. As a young man, Thompson's father flew the old mail routes down in South America, and, for a time, he worked freelance as the pilot of choice for Ernest Hemingway and Eleanor Roosevelt. Sadly, Thompson's dad passed away when Charlie was still a small boy, but he grew up surrounded by pictures of his father fishing in Key West with Hemingway, and, somehow, that sense of adventure was passed on.

The thing about Charlie Thompson is where he was living when Uncle Sam came to call: he was in Toronto, working as a scab for the daily newspaper. It was 1965, still a couple of years away from the time when thousands of young American men fled to Canada to escape service, and Thompson was already there. "I remember looking at that letter from the draft board," he says, "and thinking to myself, geez, I really don't have to go. I was living in a great part of downtown Toronto, partying every night, having a great time. I thought, why not stay here?"

But those thoughts were fleeting. Thompson had to go. It was in his swashbuckling, thrill-seeking, patriotic nature. It was in his genes. It was his duty, but equally important, it was his ticket to adventure. After a lifetime of collecting stories of his father's flying exploits, reminiscing with his father's West Point buddies, eye-balling all his dad's medals and pictures, Thompson couldn't help but be anxious to go. He must've seen *Guadalcanal Diary* and *The Sands of Iwo Jima* about a dozen times each—and that was back before video, when watching a favorite movie was hard to do.

If he had decided to stay in Canada, it wouldn't have been like he was dodging the draft, exactly, but it would have seemed cowardly to him. Despite a moment's hesitation and his convenient circumstance, he just had to sign on, and he immediately hitchhiked to Albany, New York, where he enlisted in the Marine Corps. He had it in his head that the Marines offered the best combat training, and that was what he wanted. "What the heck did I know?" he jokes now. "I wasn't basing this on anything but the impression I'd gotten from old World War Two movies, but, as it turned out, the training was tremendous. They worked us hard, but it was with a purpose. They sent me down to boot camp in Paris Island, South Carolina, and I just loved it. I loved the regimentation. I loved the guys. I loved the hard work."

Mostly, though, he loved the prospect of what lay ahead, and before he went to sleep each night, he thought of being sent overseas. He was in an honor platoon, which speaks to the kind of disciplined individual Thompson was as a young man, and it reflects his strength and abilities. He signed on for advanced training. He scored particularly well on the radio and electronics portion of his aptitude test, and, soon, he was a radio man with top secret clearance headed for a command bunker south of DaNang called Hill 55. He saw only limited action, which frustrated him. He was itching to go out on patrols, to put himself into the mix, but the folks in charge felt he had more to contribute to the effort from the relative safety of the command bunker. The truth was, Thompson was a terrific radio man, but the work only exaggerated what he was missing. All day long, all year long, he listened in over the nets to the transmissions coming back from this or that hot zone. He listened to guys getting hit and responded to crises, and he kept thinking to himself that he could do more on line duty in hot places. He could make a real difference.

And so, when it came time to leave country after his first tour, Thompson went in to see his first sergeant about returning to Vietnam for a second tour. He wasn't through, not by any stretch, but he'd had about enough of this kind of duty. "Second time around, I wanted to see combat," he says. "I made it plain. I would always be a radio man, there was no getting around it, but I wanted to be assigned to a line company. Out there in the hot spots, with guys getting hit, that's where I wanted to be."

Thompson re-upped with the 1st Battalion, 9th Marine Regiment in Dong Ha, up near the DMZ, and to hear him tell it, he handled himself pretty well. "First couple patrols, first ambush, I was scared to death," he admits, "but you get over it. What choice do you have but to get over it?" He was assigned to Delta Company as a Senior Radio Operator under the command of Captain Richard Sasek, and he was good to go. "The 'Skipper' was a great guy," Thompson remembers, "built like a Sherman tank, strong as hell, one of those super-human type guys. He really cared for his troops, but man, he was a tough mother. Built tough, too, like I said. Like he could get through anything. Like he could get all of us through anything."

A couple months into his second tour, Thompson had a chance to demonstrate the kind of heroism that would come to define his time in the military at the battle of Phu An. It was May 14, 1967, and Sasek and his men were surrounded for days by a superior North Vietnamese force. During an intense fire fight, when Thompson's Command Group and the First Platoon became separated from the Second and Third platoons, Thompson was able to radio situational reports back to the battalion command post and orchestrate an emergency medical evacuation. At one point, he fearlessly maneuvered forward under intense automatic weapon fire and rescued two wounded Marines, all the time thinking, okay, this is what I'm here for. This is why I asked out of the command post and into the field.

Now, Charlie Thompson is an intensely private man. Determined and opinionated, more times than not, he keeps quiet. Maybe all that training as a radio man in the command bunker left him holding his tongue. Whatever it is, you get the feeling he'd rather listen in than speak up. He's a powerful guy, and he carries with him a powerful presence, but much of that power is of the strong, silent variety. He keeps to himself, and about the last thing you'll catch him doing is bragging about himself in any way. Thompson's efforts at Phu An are well documented, but it's like pulling teeth to get the story from Thompson himself. When he does tell the story, he leaves out the part about receiving a Bronze Star for the calm, selfless initiative he took on that day. That part, to him, seems beside the point.

Thompson was in a crucial engagement known as Operation Buffalo, one of the bloodiest battles of the war, during which our guys suffered unthinkable casualties, and out of which Charlie Thompson emerged as the kind of selfless hero about whom people write books. (Or at least a chapter!) In the early summer of 1967, the North Vietnamese launched a major attack on a strategic marine presence at Con Thien, located approximately fourteen miles inland from the South China Sea and about two miles south of the DMZ. Con Thien was a key stronghold in the northeast corner of the region. It was also the Command Post of the 1st Battalion, 9th Marine Regiment, and the 3rd Marine Division, which were operating out of Dong Ha, about ten miles southeast.

In the days and weeks leading up to the firefight that cost him his right leg, Thompson worked to clear a six-hundred-meter wide area known as the Trace, which connected Con Thien to another stronghold at Gio Linh.

During that time, all civilians were evacuated from the area, including the abutting regions north and south of the Trace, which meant that in an attack, all bets were off. The clearing created what was known as a free-fire zone, and in this case, the zone encompassed a wide area that included several important roads and an old marketplace.

On July 2, 1967, the Trace was ripe for battle.

"It became clear, pretty early on, that they were gonna take the two base camps at Con Thien and Gio Linh," Thompson recalls of the reinforced regiment of the North Vietnamese. "That was a large number of troops, and we were outnumbered significantly, and they probably would have marched right down and taken Dong Ha, the air base. Initially, though, I don't think they really wanted to fight. Not yet, anyway. They were getting ready to stage and make their assaults on the base camps, and two of our line companies just kinda stumbled into them."

At approximately 0800 on that July morning, the Alpha and Bravo companies began moving north along Route 561, an abandoned cart road that was barely more than ten feet wide and was bracketed on both sides by thick brush. They didn't get far. Less than two hours into their sweep, the two companies were hit from all sides by artillery and mortar with such force and ferocity that they were effectively handcuffed and stopped dead in their tracks. It was like they'd run into a brick wall, overwhelmed as they were by a superior enemy force. It was a devastating attack. At one point, the North Vietnamese deployed flamethrowers to ignite the brush bordering the old cart road, effectively trapping the marines who had managed to survive the initial assault.

Thompson was sent out with a relief platoon from Delta Company, which was captained by Henry J. Radcliffe, the battalion's assistant operations officer. "Captain Radcliffe was a man on a mission," Thompson says. "He'd only been in country for about a week, had never been in combat, but he was exceptional on that day. Medal-of-Honor exceptional. Captain Sasek told me he was a good guy, and that was good enough for me."

Actually, Thompson volunteered for the assignment. He didn't want his second tour reduced to the same kind of inactivity he'd seen the first time around. As a radio man, he'd picked up the situation on the nets, knew how grave things looked for his brothers in the Alpha and Bravo companies. He wanted to get out there where he could do something about it. Plus, it didn't take a military genius to know the NVA were headed for Con Thien, where a slit trench or makeshift bunker wouldn't offer much protection on a bald hillside.

Radcliffe's group set off toward the northern perimeter of the Trace shortly after the initial attack. There were only five or six men, as Thompson recalls, with two tanks. Their mission was to find Bravo Company—and specifically, the Bravo Company commander, and to lead the retreat and evacuation of that company. The trouble was, their resources were limited, and, almost immediately, the North Vietnamese opened fire on the tiny relief force. "They had us surrounded," Thompson says, "and we didn't even know it. They could have snuffed us out without any problem, but, for some reason, they held back. I think they believed there was a larger force coming up behind us, that we were the lead party. I wish I could speak to a North Vietnamese commander from that battle, find out what they were thinking, but I'm guessing they took one look at us and couldn't possibly imagine there were just a half-dozen guys coming up with these tanks."

Soon, Thompson managed to raise a spotter plane pilot on the radio, who reported one hundred fifty or so NVA lurking in the trees to the right of the relief force. The Bird Dog directed air strikes of bombs and napalm that effectively quashed any potential threat. The air strikes killed approximately half of the NVA force and pushed the remaining troops to retreat. It was, as history has noted, a disarmingly effective stand.

As the relief force pressed north to the location of the first ambush, Radcliffe and his men encountered the dead and wounded of Bravo Company. As difficult as it was to see, it was pretty much what Thompson expected; after all, he'd heard the reports on the radio. He knew his assignment. He knew there would be dead and wounded. What he wasn't prepared for, however, was the number of marines who appeared to be shell-shocked. "Like walking zombies," is how he describes them. Guys who laid down their arms and walked blankly in the opposite direction, too shaken by what they had seen to do anything but retreat. "There was no fight left in some of these guys," he says. "They just wanted out."

And so, Thompson helped them out in what ways he could. "I'd see a body out in the field," he says, "and I'd pull 'em back, drag 'em back, whatever I had to do. We had our little blocking force out there in the DMZ, taking fire the whole time, and you could see the North

Vietnamese running around, but I was focused on getting these guys out of there. We searched the fields, the hedgerows. We looked everywhere. The heat was unbearable, must've been about 106°F, and we were running on very little water. It was a pretty mean day. The stench of the burning bodies was sometimes overwhelming. I checked every body I came across. There was no way to tell if a guy was dead or alive. The North Vietnamese had gone through and executed some of our men, shot 'em right in the head, and that was a horrible thing to see. At point blank range. That was the North Vietnamese way: that's what they did. As a senior radio man, that's what I'd hear. Our radio operators, out there in the different companies, they'd leave their voice mikes open, so I had a good picture going in, but it was nothing like seeing it for myself. Man, it was a sickening thing! It was a real hell hole out there."

That hot July day back in 1967 was hard on Thompson physically, emotionally, and spiritually. In every which way a man could be tested, Charlie Thompson was tested. And yet he came through without a scratch. He managed to pull a couple dozen marines to safety, managed to locate the bodies of a least a couple dozen more, and, throughout, he managed to maintain a level of composure that belied his circumstance. He describes his state of mind as that of "controlled chaos." He talks about being everywhere all at once and, at the same time, not being in any one place in his thinking. He says he was in a strange kind of zone.

In interviews immediately following the battle, Thompson reported that he had a single-minded sense of purpose: to save as many lives as humanly (or, super-humanly) possible. He didn't think how vulnerable he was, how exposed, how easily it would have been to be cut down in an open field as he ran headlong to retrieve another casualty under intense enemy fire. He didn't have time to think much of anything. He just acted. He wasn't alone in this, though. There was a lieutenant who had just been transferred out of Bravo Company, Gatlin Howell, who matched Thompson stride for stride, body for body, effort for effort; the men carted their wounded brothers back to the abandoned cart road with what they thought was their last ounce of strength—until another ounce was needed for the next haul. Truly, it was a remarkable, courageous display—made more so by the fact that neither man gave a thought to his own safety. Thompson can't explain it except to say that he was in that strange zone. He moved without thinking. He reacted. He did what needed to be done.

The United States forces lost many good men that day—84 killed, 190 wounded, and 9 missing—but Charlie Thompson was fine until a few days later. He was back on the line with his Delta Company crew at the dusk end of a particularly hard day of enemy shelling. The defense of the Command Post bunker at Con Thien had become an endless ordeal, and for about the third or fourth day, the marines were pounded unmercifully. "It was terrible," Thompson says. "We were stuck there in the bunker, taking hundreds and hundreds of rounds. It was almost unbelievable that we were able to withstand such force. It was just relentless. And then, all of a sudden, there was a lull in the shelling, and I stepped outside the bunker with six other marines to have a look around. The sun was going down, and we wanted to take in the scene."

It was a fairly spectacular sunset. And despite the way the shelling had devastated the countryside, there was no denying that it was a pretty place. The men admired the view, wondering how it was that such a heavenly scene could also be home to such a hell on Earth. At one point, Captain Sasek, "Skipper" to Thompson and the rest of the men in his command, gave voice to what everyone else was thinking. "Man, it's a pretty sunset," he said.

Before the captain's words had a chance to res-onate, there was a loud explosion. Whatever it was, Thompson was right in the middle of it. His body was tossed over the bunker, clear to the other side. He guesses now the impact must have thrown him about twenty feet, maybe thirty. He looked up and couldn't see a thing, not at first. There was too much dust and debris and smoke from the explosion, but he was able to see soon enough, and he wanted to close his eyes to the scene. He scrabbled over to where Captain Sasek lay alongside the much-revered First Sergeant Jettie Rivers and four other Marines. Thompson crawled over the debris without a thought for his own condi-tion. He needed to get to those men to offer what help he could, but when he pulled close, he saw that all six were dead. It was only then that Thompson gave a thought to his own injuries, and he looked down and saw that one leg had nearly been blown off. The other wasn't much better. He'd also suffered a minor con-cussion, and yet somehow he was able to put aside his own pain and offer aid to his fellow marines before worrying about himself.

The next thing he knew, Thompson was recuperating in the Philadelphia Naval Hospital, by way of DaNang, Japan, and Bethesda. Navy doctors couldn't save his right leg, which had to be amputated above the knee, but they were able to save his left leg with extensive surgeries and vein grafts. From the very beginning, he refused to think of himself as disabled. Actually, the refusal came first from the wonderful rehab nurses assigned to him in Philadelphia. "Don't think about what you *can't* do," they used to coach him, "think about what you *can* do." Thompson took the advice to heart and put himself through a rigorous rehabilitation program that continues to astound some of the disabled veterans which whom he comes into contact on a daily basis.

"You have to remember," he says, "this was back in the dark ages of prosthetics, but the folks at Philly Naval Hospital were pretty forward-thinking. They were real tough on us, teaching us to walk up steps without a rail, down steps without a rail, maximizing the strength in the muscles we had left. Nowadays, they don't push you near as hard. They've got all kinds of high-tech prosthetics, all these plastics and fibers, but they don't push you. They design these legs for people who don't want to use their muscles, but we didn't have a choice."

As a result of that early attitude adjustment from the rehab nurses, Thompson has led an active, vigorous life ever since. You'd never know he lost his leg just to look at him, except for a slight limp. He goes to the gym, lifts weights, rides his bicycle, and plays a little basketball when he can find a good game. And he tries never to get down on himself, to bemoan his situation. Sure, he's had a tough go, he'll be the first to tell you, but he's also had it better than most. He's moving about on his own power. He's got things to do, things to look forward to.

Like a lot of Vietnam-era veterans returning home from overseas, Thompson had a tough time adjusting to the change in the public perception about the war. When he left in 1966, there was still a strong, surging sense of patriotism for the effort, but by the time he returned, the mood of the country had shifted. Everyone's hair had gotten a little bit longer, everyone's morals had gotten a little bit looser, and everyone's tolerance for a war they couldn't understand had gotten a little lower. Thompson enrolled at Marshall University in Huntington, West Virginia, but he didn't have the stomach for the way people were so quick to protest the war when good people, brave people, were still over there dying. But on top of that, he found he also didn't have the head for college. He'd sit in class and his mind would wander to some of the battles he was in, to Operation Buffalo, to Phu An, and he'd run through all the different scenarios in his mind. He couldn't focus. He was focused enough to get married and start a family, but he couldn't get his mind around any kind of career, any kind of goal. He bounced around from one odd job to the next, mopping floors in a women's job corps office, working as a clerk in a liquor store, whatever came his way and seemed like a good idea at the time. He thought about quitting school.

Finally, a couple years into all this uncertainty, he was asked to speak at a Rotarian luncheon about his experiences in Vietnam. He put on a coat and tie, ran a comb through his hair, and impressed a guy in the audience who had an opportunity in mind.

"What are you doing with your life right now?" the fellow asked Thompson after his presentation.

"Not much," Thompson said. "I'm still in school, but I'm not real happy. I'd like to get started on something, to tell you the truth."

The man handed Thompson a card and introduced himself as a national service officer with Disabled American Veterans, which was dedicated to championing and preserving the rights of combat-disabled veterans. At the time, early in 1970, the DAV was one of the largest, private, non-profit service organizations in the country, and it's only gotten bigger in the years since. Thompson met up with Jesse Brown in Washington, D.C. in 1975. Later, at the Board of Veterans Appeals in Washington, they worked together handling complex appeals cases, but prior to that, Thompson was something of a road warrior. He operated first out of Winston-Salem, and then out of Buffalo, Syracuse, and the DAV's largest field office in St. Petersburg, Florida.

From that chance meeting at a Rotarian luncheon, Charlie Thompson got himself started on something, something enormously worthwhile and endlessly rewarding. "I didn't know a thing about the system when I got out of the service," he says now. "I had my own benefits taken care of, but I couldn't tell you how everything else worked. Before long, though, I could tell you anything you needed to know about Veterans

Affairs, Social Security, employment matters. I could help you navigate your way through any bureaucracy.

"I'd never really thought of it before, but I kinda stepped into something that was meant for me. I was meant to help other people. It's such a thrill. To be able to make a difference for someone, between living in the back of a car or having a home. It's such a great feeling when you get a case through like that. What more can you do than assist your fellow man? And a fellow serviceman, to boot? I can't tell you the number of times I've sat across the desk from a combat-disabled veteran, who, for whatever reason, has not filed a disability claim. The man may have been wounded a number of times, on different occasions, and, for whatever reason, he hasn't filed a claim, and you're able to look through his medical records. You're looking at the guy, looking at his records, seeing how severely wounded he was, and knowing what paperwork to submit, which claim to file, how to arrange for a medical exam. In many cases, there may have been an error in a previous filing that might date back to when he was discharged from service, and when that happens, you're entitled to all those monies in a lump sum check, and, all of a sudden, this guy's children become eligible for educational benefits, and maybe he's entitled to some sort of special housing allowance. All of a sudden, this guy goes from having nothing, or the bare minimum, to having a better life, to having what he should have had all these years, to having hope for the future. I experienced a lot of feelings in combat, but there was nothing to rival the thrill I'd get in helping a guy like this to get his life back. Nothing came close."

A LIVING HISTORY

*Alfred Pugh, Sergeant, 77th Infantry
Division, U.S. Army, World War One,
France, 1919*

Alfred Pugh

U.S. Army, World War One

At 108 years old, Alfred Pugh is very likely the old-est living combat-wounded veteran in the United States, although he bristles at the distinction. It's not the age that gets his goat, or the fact that he's outlasted all but a hearty few of his contemporaries. He minds the attention being called to a disabling injury he's spent a lifetime regarding as no injury at all.

"I took a little mustard gas is all it was," he says. "Knocked me out for a little. There's a lot of guys suf-fered a lot more than that."

Perhaps, but those numbers dwindle when set against the eighty-five years Pugh has endured lingering respiratory damage and a chronic laryngitis from inhal-ing the toxin all those years ago. He was left him speak-ing in a distinctive, hoarse whisper that sounds borrowed from an old gangster movie.

"The Lord ain't ready for me, and the devil won't have me," he teases—an easy one-liner he's adopted to explain and possibly justify his longevity.

These days, Pugh presides as something of a living legend on the nursing home wing at the Bay Pines VA

Alfred Pugh's 108th birthday on January 17, 2003, with his niece, Carolyn Layton

Medical Center in Madeira Beach, Florida, where has lived since 1996, and where he regularly regales staff, visitors, and fellow veterans with the *ear* for detail he developed when he was blinded by macular degeneration in the early 1980s. And, when he's not spinning old-time yarns or waxing political on recent world events, he's tickling the ivories—well, not the ivories, exactly, but the plastic keys of the Bay Pines organ, continuing a hobby he taught himself more than one hundred years ago. Back then, he only bothered with the black keys, in which he found more than enough melodies, but, over time, he's learned to roam the entire keyboard. On his one hundredth birthday, he entertained churchgoers at

the Aldersgate United Methodist Church in nearby
Seminole with a ten-minute medley that included "Jesus
Is All the World to Me" and "This Land Is Your Land."
In recent years, he's cut back on his playing as one of the
few concessions he's made to his advancing years.

Pugh has stories to tell: the stories of a long, long
lifetime, and there's hardly a detail lost to the years. It's
almost like a parlor trick, the way Pugh has kept his
memories close. He began working at it in earnest when
he lost his sight; he thought it would be a good mental
exercise to pass those first years in darkness by going
over the particulars of his life. He went at them sys-
tematically, year-by-year, recreating what he could,
piecing together what he could not, filing the store of
memories like snapshots in an album and revisiting and
revising to keep his mind sharp.

Pugh recalls everything. He remembers the house in
which he grew up in Portland, Maine, which was lov-
ingly built by his part-time carpenter father to accommodate his sprawling family. He remembers the
itinerant schedule of his father, who worked in a Pittsburgh steel mill half the year, commuting back to
Maine when his schedule allowed. He remembers the
first and last names of every teacher he ever had, from
the first grade on through two years of business school.
He remembers the birthdays of his six brothers and five
sisters, as well as those of the sixteen nieces and
nephews he took into his own home and cared for with
his wife of fifty-three years, Irene. He remembers the
first telephone call he ever made. And, he remembers
the French he learned as a small boy.

He was hardly alone in learning French as a child: about half the families in Pugh's hometown were of French-Canadian descent, and when he graduated from Westbrook High School in 1915, this was very much on the minds of his friends and neighbors. There was a real rooting interest in how France fared in the Great War, and Pugh and his fellows closely monitored developments overseas in what ways they could. They read about Germany's conquests at the beginning of the war and took them personally. Pugh listened to radio reports with the same fervor other young men in town reserved for their beloved Babe Ruth-era Boston Red Sox.

Pugh still listens to baseball games on the radio, but now, the hapless locals, the Tampa Bay Devil Rays, have replaced the Red Sox in his affections. Oh, and for the record, he can still tell you about the Red Sox's last World Series victory—a tightly-pitched, four-games-to-two handling of the Chicago Cubs in 1918—even though he was overseas at the time.

With such a meticulous, conditioned memory, Pugh calls to mind incidents of the Great War like they happened yesterday. He remembers how France was a "sitting duck" against the powerful German army, how France and England had yet to form a true alliance, and how the valiant French troops went wild over the news that the "Yanks" would soon join their fight.

Best of all, Pugh remembers a particularly patriotic French-Canadian girl in his high school class who used to gather the students once a week to sing the French national anthem, *"La Marseillaise."* When the students had committed the song to memory (and, to the young girl's satisfaction), it was sung at every Westbrook High School gathering, including graduation ceremonies, right alongside "The Star Spangled Banner."

Serendipitously, Pugh ran into the girl in France later on during the war. She was in a hospital near where he was stationed. She had become a nurse and wanted to work in the same part of the country where her father had been a physician, and their paths crossed in a makeshift hospital unit set up by the Red Cross. After all this time, Pugh can't get over the alarming coincidence. "You knew a girl in high school in Maine," he says, "and there she was, on the other side of the ocean."

Pugh weighs these memories and his lifelong collection of French friends against the prevailing anti-French mood of the country in the wake of the 2003 Iraqi War, and he struggles to understand the shift in the American perspective. He understands it, make no mistake, but he struggles with it just the same. He works to readjust a longstanding affinity and affection for the French people—*his* people, he once thought—against this latest turn. It used to be that he proudly wore his French Legion of Honor medal pinned to his breast pocket almost constantly, but lately he's only taken the thing out on special occasions. Of course, special occasions can take the form of a short stroll in the Florida sunshine or a visit from a reporter, but there's a taint to what had been a cherished honor.

The rest of the world has never been far from Al Pugh's reach. He gets his news from a beat-up old radio that sits by his bed, an earpiece almost permanently fitted to his ear as an accommodation to his roommate, and Pugh doesn't like what he hears. He doesn't like how, in his opinion, France has placed its financial ties to Iraq ahead of its long-term friendship with, and long-standing debt to, the United States. He doesn't like how the side of right has been obfuscated by self-interest.

"We were told that my war would be the end of warfare," he told a reporter from the *Washington Post*, who visited Bay Pines in March, 2003, to gain a cross-section of veterans' perspectives on the looming war in Iraq. "And yet here I am, the oldest living veteran of World War One, and we ain't done yet."

No, we ain't—and neither is Alfred Pugh, even though folks have been counting him out for a good

March 5, 2003. Washington Post *reporter David Maraniss interviewing Alfred Pugh in the nursing home*

long while. After his 101st birthday celebration, his first as a resident at Bay Pines, VA doctors and nurses figured he wouldn't make it to 102. But he's been racking up birthdays ever since, and he means to rack up a few more—enough, anyway, to hear the pride and might of the American flag restored to what it was when he was still a boy. God willing, there might even be a way to patch up relations with the French, and Pugh means to stick around for that day as well.

There's always been a whole lot to look forward to, is how a guy like Al Pugh accounts for his time on this Earth.

"That, and I've never stopped breathing," he jokes, but underneath the quiet gravel of his laugh, there are many learned truths: live carefully, plan ahead, take things one day at a time, and avoid uncertain paths. Back in 1915, with American involvement in the Great War anything but a certainty, Pugh signed on at the local Western Union office for a job as a telegraph operator. He has often said that if there had been a war to fight when he got out of high school, he would have signed on immediately, but, as it happened, he had a living to make. For a time, he thought it would be as a telegraph operator. From Western Union, he quickly transferred to the Maine Central Railroad in the same capacity, and he stayed with the railroad for over twenty years, returning there after his service overseas.

He enlisted in 1917 and was immediately put through some rigorous paces with his fellow soldiers. The United States Army had not fought in a war for generations, and the feeling was that the men needed time and training to be brought up to speed. For six months, Pugh's outfit slogged through mud and rain and snow and every imaginable condition, preparing for whatever they might face abroad; in France, they trained some more before joining the battle. Pugh was assigned to the 77th Infantry in France, and his face lights up when he recalls the grand welcome the American troops received when their ship came in. Thousands of French citizens lined the docks to welcome the troops, waved American flags, cheered, and sang, "Onward, Christian Soldier." Pugh remembers feeling uplifted by all the attention, but, at the same time, he also felt like a rookie up against the hardened German enemy, soldiers who'd been fighting for two to three years by then. Arriving in Verdun, he says, was a revelation; he'd heard the reports of the devastation there, but it was quite another thing to take in that devastation firsthand. "Not a single thing was left standing," he says wistfully.

First, Pugh fought as part of an American-Canadian contingent of less than one hundred men. "We were a small outfit," he says, although occasionally this small band of men made some big trouble. Regrettably, Pugh allows, it was the sort of trouble that sometimes had less to do with the war plan than it did with a group of young men letting off a little steam. Once, Pugh's regiment pulled up on the side of a hill leading down into a valley, where several railroad tracks came together in a kind of junction. On one track rested two freight cars, and word had filtered through the ranks that these cars belonged to the British army and were filled with

British delicacies. Well, that was all the young soldiers needed to hear before hatching a plan. Pugh and company had been living on a cheap brand of canned salmon that made them sick to even think about, so a few of them hit upon the idea of raiding the British stores. "It was just a prank," he says, "but we were really looking forward to those jams and jellies."

It was a prank with an unexpected kicker. Somehow, one of the intruders inadvertently released the brake on the freight car, and the next thing Pugh knew, the thing started to move. He and his buddies hightailed it out of there, and about twenty seconds later, looked back and saw a tremendous explosion. Apparently, the British supply car coasted down the hill toward another freight car at the junction that had been loaded with explosives. "They never knew it was us," he says impishly, "and we never told."

Despite such miscalculations in judgment, Pugh rose quickly through the ranks as his unit moved through the French countryside. There were only five or six months of fighting before the armistice was signed. In that time, Pugh was promoted from private to sergeant—mostly, he thinks, on the back of his strong command of the language.

"When they figured out I could speak French, they started moving me around a lot," he says. "Different regiments. Different missions. They'd wake me up in the middle of the night if they needed something translated or if they were headed off in a new direction. They'd put me out at the head of our convoys because I could read the signs. I could ask questions."

In fact, Pugh believes that the reason he took such a direct hit by the mustard gas bombardment that left him with a lifetime of respiratory trouble was because he was out in front. The Germans only hit the front part of the column and most of the men were not seriously hurt. Indeed, the Canadians took the worst of it, aside from Pugh. Mustard gas, inhaled in significant doses, can sometimes prove fatal, and, in Pugh's case, it very nearly did him in. It was the fall of 1918, and Pugh's company was positioned in the Argonne Forest. "We had no specific mission but to press forward," Pugh relates of his role in the Meusse-Argonne Offensive, one of the biggest and bloodiest battles of the war. "Our job was to push the Germans from their position, and next thing we knew they were on us with that gas."

The Americans were not caught off guard completely because they knew the Germans would very likely use the gas to protect their position. The men had been issued a primitive style of gas mask as a precaution, but Pugh remembers the thing as so unwieldy and unworkable he didn't even bother with it. "It was a rubber mask," he says, "one size fits all, and on the inside, there was a little clamp, almost like a clothespin, which I guess you were supposed to fit onto your nose. But it was so uncomfortable, and, on top of that, it didn't seem like it would offer that much protection, so I left mine behind. I wasn't too worried."

The gas left Pugh with no clear memory of the moments preceding the attack—the one stretch of time that's been lost in the long stretch of years—and knocked him unconscious for several days. French and

British medics later told him they feared for his life as they waited for him to recover. When he regained consciousness, he was itching to get back on the line. At first, doctors thought the laryngitis-like symptoms would go away over time, so Pugh wasn't too worried about his raspy voice. He wasn't too worried about the slight pain associated with deep breathing, either, because he was told that his respiratory problems would dissipate as well. What worried him, really, was the fact that he wasn't making good use of his time, that the war was marching on without him, that he wasn't being allowed to make a meaningful difference. Pugh's injuries were serious enough to warrant medical attention, but he regarded them as nothing much at all. He looked around at the men who had lost a limb, or an eye, or had suffered more apparent wounds, and he thought to himself, that's what it means to be injured. That's a ticket home. Me, that's just a scratch, nothing to keep me from rejoining my regiment.

When he was finally cleared to resume work, Pugh's first assignment was to help sort an enormous backlog of mail from the United States. The mail was being administered by the French and delivered out to the American units, but whole bags of the stuff were being lost in translation, so it was thought that the fluent Pugh could convalesce while sorting through the mess of letters and redirect them to their proper units.

Soon, he had enough of that type of work and asked to be sent back to the field, although he never did return to a combat position. He was out in the French countryside, sleeping in tents, going through some of the same motions as the active-duty soldiers, but he never again took up arms in that war. The armistice was signed just six weeks after the attack at Argonne, so there wasn't much time for Pugh to return to active duty, anyway.

He stayed in France for the better part of the next year, continuing his love affair with the country and its people. He was assigned to various clean-up patrols and worked to help stabilize the region, but he rejected his first few opportunities to come home. His voice and his breathing had yet to improve, but he was in no hurry to be examined stateside. "I was having too much fun," is how he justifies his decision all these years later. "I really enjoyed talking to the mademoiselles."

Eventually, Pugh returned to Maine and was reunited with his large family. (Two brothers also served in the Great War and returned home safely.) Having seen a war-torn France, he had no desire to visit anyplace else, and, indeed, he didn't leave his corner of New England until he lit out for Florida in his retirement years.

After the war, he took up with the railroad as if he'd never left. In 1923, he married his wife Irene, a union that lasted until her death from Alzheimer's fifty-three years later. It was a loving, sustaining relationship, although it's been Pugh's abiding regret that they never had any children of their own. But over the years, they adopted sixteen nieces and nephews and provided them with a nurturing environment when their own parents were unable to do so. None of the "adoptions" were formalized in any kind of legal sense, but the Pughs took kids in, sometimes for a few months or several years at a time. Pugh looks back on those times as some of the happiest of his long life.

"By God, I loved those kids," he says, and underneath the hoarse whisper, it's impossible to tell whether he's choking up at the memory or if it's just the mustard gas talking. The scar tissue in his throat was so damaged in by the mustard gas attack at Argonne that Pugh constantly moistens his lips when he speaks, and the gesture usually suggests a man lost in thought. For Pugh, however, it seems it's more than the gesture that gives him pause.

All those nieces and nephews kept Pugh busy as a young man, and after he'd logged his twenty years at the railroad, he thought he'd shift gears. He took a job with the postal service as a letter carrier in his rural hometown. By then, the local folks had less of a call for a telegraph operator than they did in 1916 when Pugh started out, and he figured there was more of a future in the post office. "We didn't have them fancy scooters and trucks and bicycles in those days," he says. "I did it all on foot, twelve miles a day. Snow, rain, or shine. For thirty-two years. A leather satchel on my back, filled with catalogs and packages and magazines. I'll tell you one thing, it kept me in shape."

Kept him on his toes, too. He carried dog biscuits to still the advances of local dogs and hard candy to put smiles on the faces of the children that sometimes followed him along his route. He became a fixture of his hometown and the surrounding communities.

But those days have faded into memory, and Al Pugh knows it can be a sad and wearying thing to outlast the world and people you've known. However, he chooses to look on his longevity as a blessing instead of a curse. He's outlived his wife and his brothers and sisters and most of his nieces and nephews. All of his friends from Westbrook, Maine are long gone, as are his fellow soldiers from the Great War. Too, the longer he hangs on at the nursing home, the more new friends and acquaintances come and go, but it's a routine he's gotten used to.

He sits in the darkness and smiles at his lasting good fortune. He might be blind, but he's seen a lot. He's seen some of three centuries. He's seen the development of air travel and telephone communications. He's heard all about computers and the Internet and other wireless technologies, although he doesn't have much call for that sort of thing. He's seen the days when a fellow needed a telegraphic operator to get a message through, and he's seen the days of standing on a beach with a cellular phone and calling anywhere in the world. As a boy, he looked on in wonder as his older brother, who worked for the new electric company, wired his family's home for electricity. A single, naked bulb was hung from the ceiling, and it was connected to a feeder wire that wasn't properly insulated, which young Al wasn't supposed to touch. He has marveled at the power and majesty of Teddy Roosevelt, a man who struck Pugh as smaller than he appeared in pictures when he saw him give a speech in Portland in 1907. He was embarrassed by the sordid details that surfaced during Bill Clinton's second term as president. A Bay Pines nurse recalls coming into Pugh's room during that period and asking if he was listening to the impeachment proceedings on the radio. "It's the only damn thing on," Pugh said.

In recent years, the most troubling disparity between early innovation and modern usage was the Wright Brothers' first attempts at manned flight at Kitty Hawk and the deployment of commercial jet airliners as weapons of mass destruction by Al-Qaeda terrorists. The changes that have occurred during the one hundred years of his life are hard for Pugh to comprehend. Why, just eighty-five years ago, after the Great War, the whole world loved the United States, and now Pugh hears on the radio that Americans are quietly tolerated throughout Europe and reviled in much of the Middle East. And, he can't help but wonder at the root of such a shift.

In the darkness, he chooses to hear what he wants to hear, to remember what he wants to remember, to look ahead to the promise of a world more like the one he left behind than the one he now inhabits.

THE BEST OF IT

Louis Loevsky
U.S. Army Air Corps, World War Two

Louis Loevsky isn't much for awards or citations or pats on his still-aching back, but he felt his Distinguished Flying Cross was too long in coming—fifty-five years too long, in fact.

On March 22, 1944, Loevsky's 466th Bomb Group was flying its first mission, over Berlin, when its B-24 was hit by German anti-aircraft cannons and careened into another Air Force bomber before plummeting to the ground. After years of training and months of anticipation, he was less than six hours into his first combat. As his plane spiraled out of control, navigator Loevsky performed a heroic mid-air rescue of his bombardier, who was trapped in the plane's damaged nose turret. Then both men parachuted to the city below and were immediately taken as prisoners by German soldiers—in Loevsky's case, after being severely injured in landing.

It never occurred to Loevsky or any of the survivors of the attack to put in for commendation; the true reward, each man quietly believed, came in the survival itself, in their shared ability to endure thirteen months of harsh, inhumane treatment in various German POW camps, and in the abiding camaraderie that had thrived like a virus in the harsh prison conditions and the comfort of the intervening years. But when it did ultimately occur to Loevsky's lifelong buddies to nominate him for the medal at a 1986 bomb group reunion, the Department of the Air Force initially rejected the appeal. Too much time had passed, an official maintained. Memories fade, it was suggested, and heroic stories tend to grow more dramatic with the years. A second appeal was also set aside.

On April 17, 1999, after some congressional intercession on his behalf, Loevsky was finally awarded the Distinguished Flying Cross for Heroism While Participating in Aerial Flight—one of the Air Force's highest honors. At the awards ceremony at the Air Force Heritage Museum in Savannah, Georgia, Loevsky couldn't shake the thought that the department might have gotten around to it sooner. He was honored, but, at the same time, he was put off. "It was an insulting putdown," he told a reporter from the *Newark Star-Ledger* assigned to cover the ceremony, commenting on the earlier assertion that his bomb group might have trumped-up Loevsky's valor or lost critical pieces of information to the haze of memory. "You don't forget what happened to you in war."

No, you don't, especially not if you're Lou Loevsky, a self-proclaimed packrat and inveterate correspondent who's managed to nourish an impressive list of contacts and friendships with virtually everyone who crossed his path during the war. The North Caldwell, New Jersey, home he shares with his wife Molly is strewn with the books, citations, articles, photo albums, and mementos he's assembled over the years. If it happened to him, or near him, or somewhere in relation to him, Loevsky has got a record of it somewhere. More often than not, there's a story to illuminate the record, with a budding friendship as the kicker. He's in touch with just about everybody, including his captors. He recently negotiated happy reunions with a young German woman who censored his mail when he was a prisoner at Stalag Luft 3, in Sagan, and, improbably, a young man who was part of the anti-aircraft defense battery that shot down his plane. "Sure, I was angry over what had happened," he says, "but fifty years is a long time, and, over time, some of that anger diminished. I realized we have to heal and get together."

At age eighty-three, with a pencil-thin white moustache that punctuates his great, good cheer and ready smile like an exclamation point, Loevsky appears to relish his retirement. He travels the country to visit his children, grandchildren, and a great grandchild. He also travels to reminisce with old bomb group friends that have been scattered by the years. He stands only five feet five inches tall, but he looms large among friends and family for the courage he showed in that doomed aircraft, for the composure he exhibited in completing his mission before following orders and bailing out of his plane, for the reserves of pluck and spirit and ingenuity he drew upon during those longs months in captivity at Stalag Luft 3, and for the generous, productive ways he's lived his life since returning home to his native New Jersey.

When he sits still, between reunions and dinners and vacations, he catches up on the pile of paperwork in his dining room or in his den. He organizes events, clips articles for his files, and circulates new pictures to old friends and old pictures to new ones.

Loevsky's photo albums are veritable files on the ever-graying buddies who stood at his side. He keeps mementos of the friend of a friend who did him this or that good turn, the Lyndhurst, New Jersey, neighbor who wound up in the same prison camp, the crew mate who promised Loevsky a date with Dinah Shore when they all returned stateside. He reminisces in such a way that suggests the events of World War Two have stamped him. He's lived a full life since returning home—started and sustained a family, jump-started an already successful family lamp parts business, and become a valued member of his community—and yet, underneath all of that (and a whole lot more besides), there are all those pictures. And the images form an indelible collage, which, in turn, forms the man.

Clearly, not every picture fits into an album or shoe-box or scrapbook. Loevsky keeps a picture in his mind of the moment he decided to enlist: it was Sunday, December 7, 1941, the day the Japanese attacked Pearl Harbor. Of course, he was not the only young man to enlist that day, but he believes the setting for his decision was somewhat unusual. Loevsky was at a football game at the Polo Grounds, the Giants vs. the Redskins, and when he got into his car in the parking lot after the game, the news of the attack was all over the radio. He remembers thinking it was amazing that they didn't announce it at the game over the public address system, but he guesses the authorities didn't want all that confusion, all those people getting hurt in a rush to get out of there. As it was, the parking lot was chaos.

The next day, Loevsky went down to the recruiting office in Newark. He had his heart set on the Army's Air Corps. "I wanted to be a pilot," he says, echoing the sentiments of a lot of young men of his acquaintance. "I figured, why be in the trenches when I could be in the air and have better quarters during the day? That was it for me." The recruiting sergeant had heard such thinking before, and he was prepared for it; he rolled down a big map with bright red dots indicating all the U.S. Army Air Corps installations Loevsky could consider for his training. Loevsky had spent his whole life in New Jersey, and he wasn't looking forward to another northeast winter, so he pointed to the Gulf of Mexico: Keesler Field, in Biloxi, Mississippi. He had visions in his mind of swimming, fishing, boating. The recruiting officer asked Loevsky if he'd like to put off his orders until after Christmas. Loevsky considered his Jewish upbringing and said, "Sure, why not?" He was raring to go, but happy for the few extra weeks at home, even on this false conceit.

Keesler Field turned out to be pretty much "the asshole of the United States," according to Loevsky, but he was determined to make the best of it. He didn't like that he was assigned to aviation mechanics school, either—in his head, he was already a hotshot pilot—but wanted to make the best of that, too. On weekends, to escape the doldrums of Biloxi, he hitchhiked to New Orleans, or Mobile, or Pensacola, where he stretched his twenty-one dollar monthly pay as far as his thumb allowed. He traveled lightly: shaving articles, a couple changes of underwear and socks, a couple packs of cigarettes, and a couple dollars in spending money. After approximately six months, he was shipped up to Atlantic City, and making the best of it got a little easier.

Loevsky was only one hundred thirty-five miles from home, was quartered in a hotel approximately three miles from the airfield, and reported to a captain with no on-site superiors or supporting personnel. After Keesler Field, it was almost like paradise. "We were supposed to be doing all this physical training," he says, "but there wasn't anybody really checking up on us, so we didn't put too much time in. Enough to cover the captain. We didn't march to the field, we hitched, or we hopped on the jitney. As I recall, we spent a lot of time on the beach."

Eventually, Loevsky was tapped for cadet school, but when he washed out of his pilot training, the best of it got a little tougher. "Everyone wanted to be a pilot," he reflects, "and the standards were pretty high. That comic strip, *Terry and the Pirates*, did more to inspire young men to become hotshot pilots than a Pentagon full of generals."

Terry and the Pirates, which debuted in American newspapers in 1937 and featured the exploits of fighter-pilot Terry Lee and his unsinkable band of brothers, inspired a popular radio program. The radio program, in turn, inspired many distinguished American flying careers as the United States moved toward war. As it happened, the comic strip, created by a civilian cartoonist named Milton Caniff, played a featured role in Loevsky's tour of duty as well. After receiving his navigation wings in November, 1943, in Hondo, Texas, Loevsky was deployed with the 466th Bomb Group. The B-24 to which he'd be assigned was christened "Terry and the Pirates," for its pilot, Bill Terry, and the popular Milton Caniff character. Years later, Loevsky made a particular point of befriending Caniff at an Air Force reunion gathering in Pittsburgh, and a personalized drawing of "Terry" holds a special place among his keepsakes

Before leaving for Europe, Loevsky's crew made a stop at Harrington Air Force Base, outside of Wichita, Kansas, where the men stocked up at the wholesale PX on whatever items they thought would be essential for the uncertain months ahead. "Most of the guys bought gross boxes of Hershey bars," Loevsky says. "With nuts, without nuts. It came to about a penny or two a bar. Or cigarettes. Or nylon stockings, which were becoming very popular at the time, which I guess they planned to trade for sexual favors."

Loevsky? His idea of essentials ran to a gross of condoms, which he stashed in every pocket of every one of his uniforms, meaning to keep them handy, whenever and wherever the need might arise. To this day, he doesn't know what possessed him to buy all those condoms—indeed, he didn't use a single one—but he guesses now he must have thought he could barter with them.

March 22, 1944. Loevsky and his bomb group were flying their first mission aboard "Terry and the Pirates." Their target was a BMW engine plant in Basdorf, about fifteen miles north of downtown Berlin, with the Friedrichstrasse Railroad Station in Berlin as a secondary target. The crew was told to expect moderate to heavy flak the entire way, down a corridor that stretched nearly four hundred miles from their base in Attlebridge, England. According to a press release put out by the 8th Air Force, it was to be the longest first mission ever undertaken by any American group in the European theater of operations, which was just fine with Loevsky, who was still making the best of things. It would be a challenge, the crew would rise to meet it, and at the other end, there'd be a story to tell, with pictures as reminders.

On the approach to Berlin, "Terry and the Pirates" flew in tight formation with the other bombers at an altitude of 23,500 feet. Its bombs were armed and its bomb bay doors were open; the crew would not waver from their heading. Despite the preliminary reports warning them of heavy flak, it was clear most of the way, until the group approached the IP—the initial point—which was just thirty miles north of Berlin. Loevsky began to see puffs of heavy flak above the clouds. There was a report on the radio that five hundred German anti-aircraft guns were pointed toward the skies around the city, some of them manned by women. Just then, amidst heavy cloud cover, the B-24 was hit by cannon-fire from the ground. Loevsky recalls thinking it was no wonder. "There was so much flak you could get out and walk on it," he says.

The "Terry" took a crippling shot to its first propeller. In the ensuing confusion, the plane collided with another B-24 in the twelve-ship formation, the "Brand," which was also wounded in the heavy cannon-fire. In the collision, the "Terry" sheared the tail off the "Brand," causing its sister plane to spiral out of control: eight members of the "Brand's" ten-man crew were KIA (killed in action); two parachuted to safety, only to be quickly captured by German soldiers. The "Terry" lost its second and third propellers in the impact and went into a tight spin. With just one working engine, Loevsky knew his plane would sink like a lead balloon. And it did.

Over the next tense moments, Loevsky worked valiantly to free his bombardier, Len Smith (or, "Smitty"), from the nose turret, which had been badly damaged by the plane's own propeller. The electrical and manual controls were inoperative, and, with the angle of the plane in the nose-dive, the lanky Smitty was good and trapped. "I was trying to spring the door with one hand and schlep him out with my other hand," Loevsky says. "But he was in shock, and he'd been hurt in the crash, banged his foot pretty good. I tried to get his oxygen mask on, and he kept taking it off. His gloves, too. It was about thirty-five below zero, so that's instant frostbite, and to take off your mask at that altitude, in that thin air, that could be dangerous."

Seconds turned into minutes, and Loevsky didn't have much time to spare. The order had been given to evacuate, but Loevsky wasn't going anywhere just yet, not without his bombardier. Somehow, he found the strength to wrest his buddy from the turret and direct him through the tunnel to the flight deck, where he might bail out from the open front bay. Typically, in that situation, the navigator and bombardier would have exited from the nose wheel door, but it had been bashed in by the collision with the "Brand."

Before making ready to leave himself, Loevsky released the bombs in train. "Whether it did any damage or not, I have no idea," he says. That he thought to do so at all was a tribute to his grit and determination. "Plus," he figures, "I knew we'd lost some of our guys in that collision, and I did not want it to have been in vain."

Next, Loevsky joined Smitty on the flight deck, where the bombardier was struggling with his shoes. He'd removed one of his flying boots and was trying to lace up one of his GI boots with his frozen fingers. "I looked around and saw a knit cap and scarf and a glove, and I tossed them over to him," Loevsky recalls. "I wanted nothing but for him to get the hell out of there. Go, I'm thinking. Just, go! I almost booted him out of the plane, and when he bailed out he was hold-ing one shoe, one boot, a scarf, a glove, a cap."

As Loevsky made ready to bail out himself, he saw his pilot, Bill Terry, standing at the control column. The plane was probably at about nine thousand feet at that point, and dropping fast, and Terry was mak-ing some last minute adjustments. He hollered across the flight deck to Loevsky. "Hey Lou," he said. "Wait for me."

Loevsky waited until Terry crossed from the control column to the bomb bay, and, at that point, he bailed out. A moment later, while he was still free-falling, he looked up and saw a parachute opening above him and assumed it was Terry's, but that was the last Loevsky ever saw of his pilot and friend. According to the missing air crew report, the Germans later claimed to have found four bodies in the plane after it crashed; a fifth body, Bill Terry's, was found about five hundred meters from the plane. Loevsky always believed (but never confirmed) that Terry was shot out of the sky as he parachuted to Earth. In all, five airmen escaped the "Terry."

The 466th Bomb Group had no actual parachute experience, just a half-hour or so of classroom instruction and what Loevsky calls "do not" theory, as in: *do not* collapse the chute, *do not* touch the shroud lines, *do not* leave your chute where the enemy might find it once you reach the ground. At that point, Loevsky would have settled for reaching the ground, period. "Basically, they taught us to clear the plane and pull the rip cord and hope for the best," he says.

And so, once again, Lou Loevsky intended to make the best of it. He went into a long free-fall, thinking it the best course against the potential of enemy aircraft or enemy ground fire. "I didn't trust the bastards," he says. "One of the things they had time to teach us was that you could collapse a chute just by coming too close to a plane. They don't even have to scrape you. The slipstream alone can collapse the chute, and I just figured the longer I was floating down to the ground, the longer I'd be a target, and the bigger target I'd be, so I stayed in that free-fall for as long as I could."

Falling, he was overcome by how quiet and peaceful it was up there at altitude, especially compared to the noise and confusion of just a few moments earlier. It was like someone had switched off the volume. He stretched out horizontally and cupped his chin in his hand, like a scene out of a cartoon. He watched the ground slowly come up. As he fell, his mind raced. He thought of the dog tags he wore around his neck, with an "H" marking him as Jewish. He wondered why the

Army even needed a religious designation on his tags, and then he realized that it was to ensure that if he were killed, he would receive a proper burial. Still, he hardly went to synagogue unless he was invited; he'd been to a few bar mitzvahs, weddings, funerals, but he wasn't what you'd call observant. For all practical purposes, he considered himself a secular Jew, and there he was, free-falling into German territory, where if he was identified as such, he likely would have been killed. "For this I needed an 'H' on the dog tags?" he asks. "So now the question becomes, do I leave the tag on or rip it off and throw it away? All this is running through my mind as I'm falling. And then I realized that if I was caught without tags, I risked being shot as a spy. No dog tags, you're a spy, right? Some choice. Leave it on and risk being shot as a Jew, take it off and risk being shot as a spy. So I figured I'd take my chances and leave it on."

His next thoughts ran to all those condoms stuffed into all those pockets in all those uniforms—including the one he had on! He worried that the condoms would wind up with his personal belongings after he died. Someone would place them in his footlocker and send them home to his parents, and they'd be left wondering what kind of sex fiend they'd raised.

His emotions ran from uneasiness to anger. Actually, it was anger most of all. He says now he was too stupid or charged up to feel any fear, and focused instead on being angry at himself for getting shot down before having had a chance to make a real contribution to the war effort. It was his first mission, after all, and now it appeared it would also be his last.

At about four thousand feet, still in free-fall, Loevsky spotted two small garrisons down below. He had no choice but to pull his ripcord. If he waited any longer, there wouldn't be time for his chute to open. The chute quickly filled, and in the stillness of the sky, he took full notice of the commotion on the ground. In one of the camps, the men appeared to be shooting at Loevsky; in the other, they appeared merely to be pointing, so he did what he could to steer himself in the direction of the pointing. "We'd been taught not to touch those shroud lines," he says, "but I became an instant expert at maneuvering that parachute. I slipped. I spilled. Slipping is to change directions. Spilling is to reduce the amount of air, the size of the chute, but you're going like a bat out of hell. Hit the ground like that and your knees will go through your shoulders."

A resourceful Loevsky managed to slip and spill away from the shooting, toward a small tree he managed to pick out on a downtown street. He briefly thought it strange that there was a tree reaching up out of the concrete—like *A Tree Grows in Brooklyn*, he thought—but he didn't have time to question what he took to be his good luck. He was plummeting so fast that he could have broken every bone in his body on landing—if he even survived the landing. At least the tree would break his fall. He crossed his legs "for posterity," he says, and braced for the impact, taking out one side of the tree as he crashed through its branches. The chute snared on one of the upper limbs, and Loevsky was flipped in the tug and pull, his feet whipped over his head, and his back thrown to where it would never be right again.

He blacked out.

"I don't know how long I was out," he says, "but I don't think it was too long. When I came to, there was a gun in my ribs. I was hanging from the tree, just an inch or so off the ground. My toes could touch, but my heels could not. It's like I was bouncing. There was a wrenching pain in my lower back. And here was this *Volkstrum*, this elderly civilian home guard, all dressed in black, sticking his gun in my ribs and shouting, '*Pistole? Pistole?*'"

Two *Wermacht* troops quickly arrived and took control over the home guard, but before Loevsky could unhitch himself from his parachute harness, three SS soldiers joined them. The troops began to argue over authority. Loevsky's parents had often spoken Yiddish in his house, and he knew enough of the language to pick up what was being said in German. Each group wanted custody of the American prisoner, and Loevsky kept quiet as his fate was determined. If the SS prevailed, he knew he'd likely be sent off to a concentration camp and killed. With the *Wermacht* troops, he thought he might stand a chance. He didn't like his odds either way.

Ultimately, the *Wermacht* troops prevailed, and the three storm troopers took off in a huff as Loevsky was finally separated from his harness and marched through the streets of Berlin. There was a German soldier on each side of him, and as they proceeded to their headquarters, the locals shouted for Loevsky's neck. "It was like a lynch mob," he says now, "and if it wasn't for those two *Wermacht* troops drawing their sidearms to keep the mob at bay, they'd have strung me up right then and there."

Loevsky found Len Smith at the *Wermacht* headquarters, along with Joe Greenberg, his flight engineer.
He couldn't figure out how Smitty had managed to pull
his ripcord because he was still holding his hat, his
scarf, his gloves, one boot, and one shoe. His hands
were swollen and purple due to frostbite, and his foot
had been badly injured in that nose turret, but he was
alive. For weeks afterward, Loevsky convinced some of
the other prisoners to hoard some margarine from their
rations for Smitty, which he used as a kind of salve, and
he managed to keep his hands.

Airmen were sent to a special interrogation camp,
where they were strip-searched and processed as prisoners. Once again, Loevsky had good reason to fear for his
life. He worried that his circumcised penis would mark
him as a Jew, but more than that, he worried about being
separated from his electrically heated flying suit. It was
winter, and it was cold enough with the damn suit on; he
couldn't face a transport to a prison camp in open boxcars in the dead of winter without his heated gear. So what
did he do? "I pulled rank on 'em," he says. "They were
GIs. I was an officer. I started sounding off, loud and clear,
in English, as if they could understand. What the hell was
I thinking? A small, naked, circumcised, Jewish boy, risk-
ing God only knew what. But they handed me back that
suit, I'll tell you that. And I was damn glad to have it."

The Germans did confiscate the heating elements
from the suit when Loevsky arrived at Stalag Luft 3 in
Sagan, but he took his small victories where he could
find them. As it was, he was suffering from a debilitating
back pain from his parachute landing, and the pain was

worsened by the constant butting of German rifles to keep him moving along in line. He feared that without medical attention, the pain would get worse.

"Terry and the Pirates" was shot down several days prior to the legendary "Great Escape" at Stalag Luft 3, and by the time Loevsky was transported there with his "purge"—a new group of POWs (or, "kriegies," for the German *kriegsgefangenen*)—the mood of the prisoners was decidedly upbeat. Seventy-six of their own had just managed a daring and inventive tunneling escape, and the *kriegies* allowed themselves to think their situation a little less bleak. The dramatic escape, later chronicled in the bestselling book, *The Great Escape*, by Paul Brickhill, and a Hollywood movie of the same name, turned out to be somewhat less successful than the prisoners had originally been led to believe. Within days of Loevsky's arrival in camp, word came down that fifty of the seventy-six escapees had been shot and killed by German soldiers on the direct orders of Adolph Hitler; twenty-three had been recaptured and placed in "the cooler," to be reassigned to other prison camps; only three prisoners made good on their escape and remained at large. Morale plummeted. A senior American officer gathered the prisoners in the center compound to offer this assessment. "Gentlemen," he announced, "we are helpless and hopeless."

But Loevsky was undaunted. He'd only just arrived at the prison camp, so he'd yet to experience the full extent of its inhumanity, but he likes to think he would have taken a positive view if he'd been a camp veteran as well. Three men had escaped, and, to Loevsky, that was cause for celebration and reason for hope. Years later, he met and befriend Dr. Bram Vanderstock, a veteran of the Royal Dutch Air Force, and at the time, the only living escapee. Loevsky reports that Vanderstock was fascinated to learn how his exploits impacted the other prisoners, both in good ways and bad. Of course, Vanderstock regretted that after his escape the prisoners were subjected to frequent and thorough Gestapo searches and otherwise harsh treatment, but he was uplifted by the prospect that his daring offered even a slim ray of hope to some of the men.

The conditions at Stalag Luft 3 were brutal, as Loevsky soon discovered. The prisoners slept two hundred men to a barracks in sixteen-man bunks stacked four high, with little or no food and little or no warm clothing in winter months. The conventional measure was that *kriegies* would lose about a pound a day for the first three months or so, until they were down to mostly skin and bones. Whatever they had to eat, they shared. At night, the talk was not of women or the comforts of home, but of food. Each prisoner was supposed to receive a Red Cross parcel of rations each week, but the Germans constantly claimed that looters raided the Red Cross trains. The prisoners were placed on half rations or quarter rations—or, for a long stretch over the winter, one-eighth rations.

"We took turns slicing the bread," Loevsky says, "and the man that did the slicing got the last slice, so you could be sure everyone got an equal cut."

The food was so bad, he reports, that some men chose to do without, at least for a time. To better make his point, Loevsky lapses into a cherished yarn. One night, a new *kriegie* was assigned to Loevsky's combine, and he sat down at the table wearing his officer's hat with a fifty-mission crush at a jaunty angle. Loevsky remembers the officer as somewhat cocky, and he looked at the food on the table with great distaste: ersatz coffee, which was made from roasted acorns; "goon" bread, which tasted like it was made from sawdust; and a ghastly looking piece of meat. The officer had not yet spoken, then he indicated the meat at the center of the table and asked, "What the hell is that?" Someone explained that it was *blutwurst*, allegedly made from the blood of slaughtered animals mixed with sawdust. The officer pushed his share aside and announced, "I'd sooner eat shit." The very next night, that same officer returned to the same table, humbled and hungry. He meekly gestured to plate of *blutwurst* at the center of the table and said, "Please pass the shit."

Loevsky guesses he must have told that story a hundred times over the years, and, in each retelling, there are traces of the resolve and resilience that saw him through. He made the best of it over and over again. He was a resourceful sort. He built and tended his own garden, with seeds supplied by the YMCA, complete with a jerry-rigged irrigation system that gave him something to look forward to each day, until the Germans put an end to it. *"Das ist verboten!"* he'd hear, and that would be that.

He helped to organize the methodical removal of the sub-flooring in his barracks, using the crawl space beneath to store contraband and avoid inspection.

He rigged a stick with a bent nail and a knife to "harvest" the dandelions growing between the guard rail and an electrified fence, which the members of his combine ate raw, cooked (if possible), or mixed into a salad. The effort proved so successful that he soon made modifications and began using the device to snare all kinds of fresh vegetables. *"Das is verboten!"* he heard again, after he and his buddies had helped themselves to a few extra meals.

He collected newspaper tear sheets with pictures of Adolph Hitler and made sure to bring these to the "abort," for his weekly bowel movement. (There wasn't enough fiber in his diet to call for more frequent trips.) "We POWs had so little fun," he says. "Using Hitler's press clippings as toilet tissue helped to make my *kriegie* existence more bearable."

He collected empty Red Cross cartons and tore them into long, curly strips of cardboard, which he then threw into a purloined mattress cover. The other officers in his combine didn't know what to make of their friend, tearing away at all the cardboard, hour after hour, day after day, until the pile was reduced to a down-like consistency. When the mattress cover was fairly filled, Loevsky found some waxed string and bits of scrap leather and tufted it to make a comforter. The thing kept him so warm, he said, he was able to trade his threadbare German-issued blanket—but not before cutting off a swatch and using it to fashion a hood, a scarf, and a pair of mittens. Some months later, in the days-long "march" from Stalag Luft 3 in Sagan to Stalag 7A in Moosburg, the blanket, hood, scarf, and mittens came in handy as the prisoners were transferred in a freezing blizzard, crammed into boxcars like swine.

Once, after realizing that only the hardiest men took cold water baths in winter, Loevsky thought to put the surplus soap to use as fuel. He dumped a box full of soap into his barracks stove, which huffed and puffed and let out thick columns of dense, black smoke—and tremendous heat, besides.

"I always had a project going," he now recalls. "It kept me sane and allowed me to focus on something other than our ordeal. The others used to think I was a little crazy. They'd say, 'Oh, that Lou, he's around the bend again,' but a lot of these little projects made our lives there more bearable, and when they didn't help in that regard, they at least made things a little more interesting."

Loevsky won't suggest that time flew by during his 404 days of captivity, but he bit the bullet and made the best of it—like most everyone else, he says. There was nothing else to do but tough it out. On the day of his liberation, April 29, 1945, he stood less than fifteen feet from General George Patton, who rode through the Moosburg camp in the lead tank in his pressed battle jacket, polished helmet, and spit-shined boots, presenting a stark contrast to the bedraggled, beaten-down prisoners. Loevsky was numb and bone-tired, and he'd yet to receive any medical treatment for his back injury—a condition that continues to plague him all these years later—but he was momentarily lifted by the spectacle.

He was free, at last. He was going home.

It's the years since that have passed quickly, Loevsky says. Rebuilding his family business. Raising his family. Finding love and happiness a second time, with his second wife, Molly. Keeping tabs on his old pals from his bomb group, and setting the record straight on what it was really like in those German POW camps. Sorting through the endless pile of memories, reattaching old names to aging faces, finding the familiar in a forgotten photograph.

Perhaps the most compelling moment of Loevsky's post-war freedom came fifty-five years after his liberation, when he was "reunited" with a retired German hotel manager named Harry Schuster, who tracked down Loevsky to apologize for having shot down his plane with his 88 mm anti-aircraft battery. The two veterans

Leonard Smith (left) and Louis Loevsky (right) in Moosburg, Germany, two days after liberation by General Patton, April 29, 1945

corresponded warily for some months before agreeing to a get-together with their wives at a hotel in Council Bluffs, Iowa. Schuster had only been sixteen years old when Loevsky's bomb group filled the skies over Berlin. All of the city's schools had been closed, and the young males were recruited for anti-aircraft work. Schuster recalled seeing Loevsky's disabled bomber head directly for his gun position on the ground then crash in a park across the street. The young Germans were forbidden to leave their positions, but Schuster and a friend took off to see the wreckage, camera in hand.

A German soldier guarding the wreckage of Terry and the Pirates

Sadly, Schuster died suddenly just weeks after the unlikely reunion, but Loevsky keeps the picture Schuster took on that gray March day in Berlin. A helmeted German soldier stands astride the twisted wreckage of "Terry and the Pirates," and caught in that still frame is the essence of Loevsky's time in the service, his time in captivity, and his time living with the specter of each.

"We were just young men, doing what we were told," he says, with the perspective of a half-century. "Who's to say who shot who? There were six other cannons in his battery. I couldn't hold this man accountable, but I could shake his hand and put the past behind us and move on."

And, he could pose for yet another picture—of two, creaky veterans willing to bury their pasts and look ahead to better times.

Lou Loevsky and Harry Schuster

DOWNHILL RACER

Chad Colley
U.S. Army, Vietnam War

S ome guys are hard-wired to persevere. No matter
what. No matter when. No matter how. Deal them
a lousy hand and they'll play it to advantage or, at least,
in the best way they know.

For Chad Colley, a triple amputee who lost both
legs and a forearm in an explosion in the hedgerows of
Vietnam, who went on to earn his pilot's license and
two gold medals in the 1992 Para-Olympic games in
Albertville, France, the best way he knows is the only
way he knows. He's built a successful career as a real
estate broker in his Arkansas hometown, served as the
national commander for Disabled American Veterans,
and been honored by President Ronald Reagan as the
Handicapped American of the Year. Colley's many and
varied accomplishments are enabled by the kind of
hard-wiring that runs beyond perseverance to hope and
faith, pride and purpose, endless enthusiasm, and
boundless good cheer.

"I had about twenty seconds in there, right after I
was injured, when I went through every conceivable
stage of grief," he says, matter-of-fact about the blast

that claimed his military career and nearly took his life in the bargain.

Spending even a few minutes in his winning company, with his full-wattage smile, neat trim of white hair, and the kind of cut upper body that comes from a full lifetime of asking his arms to do the work his legs used to do, reveals that there's no braggadocio about Chad Colley. Without bluster or conceit, he's just an unassuming man who assumes people expect to hear the truth out of him, without varnish. And he delivers: "I went from being angry, to wanting to die, to wanting to live, to wanting to live *fully*, all before a single person laid a hand on me. It's amazing how quickly your mind can work, when you're up against it."

Chad Colley was no stranger to *up against it* when he enlisted in 1966, straight out of military college. His father had been a career soldier, indeed, a veteran of World War Two, Korea, *and* Vietnam. Colley had his heart set on following in his path. He spent his youth following his father around the globe, so it's no wonder; Colley logged parts of his childhood in Germany, Japan, Georgia, and Kansas, with most American summers spent surrounded by his extended family in Arkansas. It was, to hear him tell it, a decidedly positive experience, vagabonding from one base to the next, making new connections, and, before too terribly long, moving on. Happily, the only time Colley managed four consecutive years in the same school happened to coincide with his high school years, in Columbus, Georgia, but he guesses all of that stopping and starting made him a more adaptable person, more outgoing, more open to new experiences than he otherwise might have been. Anyway, he wouldn't have traded it for the world.

"It wasn't like you were going into a totally new place," he says. "You were alone, but you weren't completely alone, if you know what I mean. You were surrounded by all these other people experiencing some of the same things. People who had already gone through the same process, who were looking ahead to more of the same. I don't know anyone who really relishes change, but I didn't mind it. I truly didn't. And I don't mind it now."

Colley was eight years old when he decided he wanted to be a soldier. In some ways, the decision had almost nothing to do with his father—not directly, not at first—although Colley looks back and guesses it had everything to do with the man his father had become and the life he'd built for his family. It was what Colley knew, after all.

The spur to decide was an unexpected brush with military history taken in by the wide eyes and open heart of a child. Colley's family was living in Fort Riley, Kansas, which is an old cavalry base where most of the main buildings were laid out in grand style. One of the grandest buildings is an historical residence that had been occupied by General George Custer when he was stationed at Fort Riley. During Colley's time there, the honor of living in that house was given to a Congressional Medal of Honor winner named Robert B. Nett. Nett, it so happened, was an old friend of Colley's father, and, one evening, the Colleys were invited over to the famous Custer house for dinner.

"We're driving over there," Colley recalls, "and, like fathers will do, my dad said we could talk about anything with his friend except his Medal of Honor. He told my brother and me not to bring it up, and, of course, that was all I needed to hear. It took but about four minutes for me to broach the subject once we arrived, and this man couldn't have been nicer about it. He took me upstairs to his bedroom and opened his bureau and took out his medal and hung it around my neck. And then he repeated to me some of the same things President Truman had told him when he put it around his neck during the Korean War. Something about how our country will be free and be a light to the world as long as men were willing to make the sacrifice that he had made. Words to that effect, and I took them to heart because from that time on, I just thought being a Medal of Honor winner was as good as it could possibly get."

And so, Colley heard the call to service. It had been a possibility all along, but it took that Medal of Honor around his neck to get him clear on it. Soon, it was all he could think about. He started going to the pistol range with his father, and, by the age of ten, he could field strip every single weapon his father brought home for his inspection, all the way down to a .45. His idle moments were filled with thoughts of leading men into battle, and jumping out of airplanes, and sleeping in tents. He had it all figured out, so when it came time for college, he enrolled at North Georgia College, a military institution where the students wore uniforms and followed a chain of command. There, Colley got his first taste of regimented routine. He studied mathematics and physics, not because he had any great love for the subjects or any particular talents in that direction, but he wanted to earn an Army commission as a second lieutenant, and he figured this course of study would bring him closer to his goal. This was what he wanted, and this was what it took. It was what he knew, after all.

When he graduated in 1966, there was no question where Chad Colley was headed. (Actually, he was known as Ralph Colley back then, same as his father, but when he came home from Vietnam, he took the initial C that stood in for his middle name and made it Chad.) He moved through the Airborne Ranger School at Fort Benning, Georgia, like it had been designed with him in mind, and then went on to the 101st Airborne Division in Fort Campbell, Kentucky. He was on a fast track toward making a difference, itching to get over to Vietnam at a time when it was still widely thought that a full-scale U.S. engagement would put a swift end to the fighting. There were some days when Colley thought our troops would wrap things up in Southeast Asia before he ever got a chance to do his thing, and he couldn't race through his training quickly enough.

"I was always in very good physical shape," he says. "Not to say it wasn't rigorous, because they really put it to you, but I was up to it. Some of the guys, though, they got to thinking if the Department of the Army knew what these instructors were doing down there in Ranger School, then somebody would have it handed to them. Little did we know that everything had its purpose. The sleep deprivation, the physical activity. Everything helped you to move beyond what you thought were the absolute limits of your ability and endurance, teaching boys to be men.

"If you went on a patrol and somehow blew your mission, they wouldn't let you eat for two or three days, and you'd think, well, how can they do this? Or, you'd get back to your tent after a full day and think you had time to rest, and the next thing you know, you're going out on a five-mile run. You had to strike your tent, load your gear, put everything on your back, and run five miles after you just spent about twenty hours in the field. And again, you'd think, oh, this can't be right. But what I learned from the experience was that the human body is capable of so very much more than you can possibly imagine. You can really be at your best when you're really pushed against it, and knowing that benefits you in everything you ever do in life. I mean, you learn that your absolute limit is not, in fact, your absolute limit. That limit is not met until you just absolutely collapse. And as frustrating as it might have been when I was in the middle of it, it's served me well in many, many instances, when I've thought about giving up, when I've tried and tried and given it my best shot and it's just not working out. And I'd just reach down and grab one lower gear and go one more time. You realize it's that one more time that makes the difference."

When Colley joined the 101st Airborne Division, he expected to stay in Kentucky for approximately a year. The 101st was divided into three brigades, and up until then, only one brigade was detailed to Vietnam at a time, so the loose plan was for Colley to continue with his training at Fort Campbell until his brigade was rotated overseas. Personnel guessed that would be in June, 1968. However, late in 1967, as the fighting escalated, the decision was made to accelerate that plan, and Colley was told he'd be shipping out months ahead of schedule. The change left Colley to bump up his long-planned wedding to his college sweetheart, Betty Ann; the couple had thought they'd have a year or so until Colley rotated out of Fort Campbell, but they made hasty rearrangements to get the ceremony in before the groom was sent overseas. Betty Ann, a physical therapist, was herself the child of a military marriage—her father had been in the Army Air Corps during World War Two—so she knew what she was getting into.

"She knew parts of it, anyway," Colley says. "To tell you the truth, I don't think I had a complete idea what I was getting into."

Six weeks after the wedding, Colley's orders came through, and on Thanksgiving Day, 1967, he left with his brigade for the front. He had a whole lot for which to be thankful. His active military career was about to begin after pretty much a lifetime of training, and his beautiful young bride would be waiting for him back home, so he loaded up on turkey dinners at every opportunity. He had one feast at Fort Campbell complete with the all the trimmings before boarding the C-141 army plane that took him out to Anchorage, Alaska; he had another meal in Alaska, and a third Thanksgiving dinner at a stopover in Japan. By the time he set down in country, he was fat and happy and itching to get going.

Base camp was at Phouc Vihn, approximately fifty miles northwest of Saigon. Colley was assigned a platoon of approximately forty men. He was twenty-three years old, and he remembers thinking, it's about time. He'd imagined that day since he was eight years old, and he was careful to take it all in. He didn't want to miss a single aspect. His first and lasting impressions of Vietnam were that it was very hot and that there was a distinctive smell about the place. "It was extremely humid," he recalls, "almost stifling, and on top of that, there were all these strange odors, smells you wouldn't necessarily associate with anything good."

The first order of business was to acclimate to the weather and conditions of the region, to transpose the textbook learning from back home to the uncertain circumstances of the field. Colley says it wasn't always easy, running training programs designed to shift the focus from drills to the real deal, but it was a necessary transition. He must have done a good job of it because after six months, he was made company commander and put in charge of many men far older than he was. He took the promotion in stride and the attendant responsibilities very much to heart. "To me," he says, "the greatest single accomplishment that you could achieve over there was taking the mission you were presented, implementing it successfully, and getting through the night without getting anyone hurt or killed. I mean, that was just a real heady thing, whenever you could do that."

He says: "Out in the field, we were usually resupplied late in the afternoon, around three or four o'clock, and that was when the men would normally eat. But as a company commander, I was too busy to eat at that time. There were too many things to do. I had to implement our mission, decide where to put listening posts and so forth, worry over ambushes and fallback positions, know where the other units were. You better believe it, there was a lot going on. By the time we were ready to move into our night defensive position, I still would not have eaten, but I had to go around and make sure all the fields of fire were appropriate with our machine guns and all that. Finally, about nine o'clock or so, I'd be ready to eat, but, of course, over there, we heated our meals with a little chunk of C-4, and you don't burn fires in Charlie's backyard at night. So there was some degree of sacrifice, but that was all well worth it the next morning, when the ambient light would get bright enough that you could differentiate between a tree and a person. That sun would come up and you'd have that great, heady sense of accomplishment again, of getting through the night without getting someone hurt."

July 21, 1968. Colley had been in country for approximately eight months, out in the field over two weeks, and was just resupplied. His company was due to rotate back into base camp later that day, and they were approximately ten kilometers from their pick-up point, with attachments in tow: two 81 mm mortar crews from E Company and the Battalion Recon Platoon. Colley says his guys were so anxious to get back to base camp that they covered those ten kilometers in just about an hour and fifteen minutes, double-time.

"They were ready to rock 'n' roll," he says. Indeed, they were so eager to get back to base camp that they arrived at the pick-up point ahead of their rendezvous. As they waited, Colley's radio operator began catching conversation about a firefight not too far from their position. The guys in earshot grew concerned—none more than Colley. "When you're shifting positions like that and fixing to leave and something happens to one of your other units, it's never a good thing," he says.

A plan emerged. Six rifle companies—approximately 750 men—would cordon off the area under fire. Colley's company would be the last of the six to be put into position. He was given the coordinates by his battalion commander, and, moments later it seemed, they were set down approximately one kilometer from where he and his men were to close the gap in the barricade. He'd been in battles before, so he knew what to expect, which basically meant he'd have no idea what to expect.

"We were the last ones in, so we were making time," he says, "but, at the same time, we were making certain, you know. I had those attachments in trail behind my company, just to make for better command and control. The particular area we were moving through was one of the more difficult types of terrain to cover in Vietnam. Old garden plots, primarily. Square- or rectangular-shaped fields bordered by low mounds of dirt that had grown thick with bushes and trees, like a hedgerow. You couldn't see to the other side, which made the fields like huge checkerboards, running for miles in every direction. The only way to secure an area like that was to travel it in a column of two long lines, each man approximately five or six meters from the one in front, each column about twenty meters apart."

There was a full platoon out in front, and Colley followed with the next group; he wanted to keep close. The company moved swiftly through the hedgerows, mindful of the booby traps they'd likely encounter on the way to their position. There was evidence of such traps here and there: a torn U.S. Army uniform, a stock of an M-16 that had been exploded.

Colley can still picture the scene in his mind. He's got a fixed image of his position, the position of his men, the position of their target. It's stayed with him all these years, he thinks, because it's his last clear picture before whatever the hell it was that happened next. He went from that clear, detailed picture to an eerie, almost somnambulant silence. Boom, in the space of an instant. All of a sudden, it was deathly quiet, where just a moment before there'd been chatter and orders and commotion. Colley was dimly aware of debris raining down around him. There was a swarm of dust. He tried to process what it was he was seeing, feeling, hearing. He tried to stand, but he couldn't; he tried to raise himself up on his elbows, but he couldn't manage that, either. He looked down and saw that his legs were gone at the knee, and he wondered what that might mean. He noticed his thighbone, on the left side of his body, exposed from the knee to his hip, and it struck him as very, very white. That's what registered, the whiteness of it.

He suffered a concussion in the blast, but he wasn't out more than a couple seconds, as best he can figure.

As he inched past the numbness and confusion and made a kind of sense of his situation, he became angry. Really, that was his first, most intense emotion: anger at himself. He lay in a hole in the earth made by whatever it was that had gone off at his feet, a pool of his own blood forming around his wounds, and was pissed off at himself. Mightily. He thought to himself, you're the company commander! You're the leader of all these men! You knew something like this could happen! You walked right into it!

"It wasn't any time at all before someone came to my side," he says, "but it was all the time I needed to absolutely plumb the depths of that anger. Probably no more than fifteen seconds, and, in that time, I went through every one of those stages of grief that you read about. It all happened for me right there in that hole. I was furious at myself. That hit me first. Then, when my situation became clear, I wanted to die. I didn't know the full extent of my injuries, or what the consequences would be of those injuries, but at just that moment, they seemed overwhelming. I plain wanted to die, and I was content with that decision. It registered, and I was okay with it, and then I started looking at it in a new way, and I moved from wanting to die to wanting to live. Just like that. I still didn't know what the future might hold for me, what kind of shape I was in, but I wanted to live, and then I tried that on for a while, another couple seconds, looking at what all that might mean, and I was content with this decision, too. It felt right. And then it wasn't enough to merely survive what had happened, so I made another decision. I decided to really live, to make myself whole, whatever it took. All in that first half-minute or so."

Colley may not have realized it at the time, but it was his training kicking in. He'd been pushed to his absolute limit and been forced to grab for that one lower gear, to go one more time. There was a soldier out in front who'd been hit in the blast, and another soldier behind Colley in the column had taken some shrapnel as well, but neither was as seriously wounded. For the longest time, Colley thought he'd stepped on a mine in the field, but a couple of the men subsequently found wires running into the dirt, disappearing in the hedgerows, which suggested that it was a command-detonated mine: Charlie had been laying in the bushes some distance away.

Colley lapsed quickly into a state of shock, and after those first clear moments, there's a good deal of time lost to dust and confusion. He never lost consciousness, but there was a time or two in there when someone had to slap his face to get him to focus or respond to a question. He has a few specific memories: a couple medics holding blood expanders and making a shadow across his face as small relief against the searing sun; the wonderful smell of the jet fuel from the helicopter; the surgical team, with their green scrubs, masks, and upraised gloved hands; his own reflection, nine times over, in the makeshift lighting unit of the MASH operating theater.

And yet for every crystal clear memory, there are moments he might never recover. At a company reunion thirty-five years later, one of Colley's men revealed a telling detail. "He told me the most amazing thing," Colley says. "Apparently, before I passed out, I called my senior platoon leader and officially handed the company over to him. I have no recollection of that, but this man swears to it. Said the men couldn't get over it, someone in that kind of shape, going by the book like that."

Through e-mails, letters, and follow-up accounts, and through his own recaptured memories, Colley's been able to build a kind of timeline of what happened next. On that day, for the only time during his tour as company commander, Colley had been traveling with those two mortar crews attached to his company. The battalion reconnaissance platoon was headed with Colley's unit for the same position in the six-company barricade up ahead; the medic for the recon platoon was the senior medic in the battalion, serving his second tour in Vietnam, and he immediately moved toward Colley to assess his condition. At the same time, Colley's company medic, a close friend with whom Colley would share taped messages and care packages from home, was also racing to his side. The company medic arrived first, but he froze at the site of his good buddy all busted up like that.

"He was like a deer in the headlights," Colley says, "which I could certainly understand. I mean, this man had seen a lot of significant injuries, worse than what had happened to me, but I was his friend. Doesn't matter what your training tells you, it's different when there are emotions involved, and he kind of dropped his pack when he got a good look at me. His jaw dropped, too. This other medic, the recon platoon medic, he comes running up behind and takes over. You know, I don't mean anything to him, I'm just another piece of meat in green, and he gets to work, applying tourniquets and rousing my company medic into action, and doing what he had to do. They couldn't get a tourniquet on my left leg, the way it was tore off, so they had to use as much compression as possible to staunch the flow of blood. The whole time, I'm talking up a storm. Another one of my guys, he told me later I just wouldn't shut up. Talking about my wife, about how she was a physical therapist, how this was her big deal, taking care of guys in this kind of shape. I was just going on and on."

Colley doesn't remember feeling any pain until he was on the Medivac being choppered the fifteen minutes to the nearest MASH unit. He was on a canvas stretcher which was bowed by his body weight, and when they set him down on the metal floor of the helicopter, he could see a river of blood run from his stretcher, where it was pooling, to just under the pilot's seat. He thought to himself, this is not good. This just can't be good. One of the medics started using an air bag to try and force air into Colley's lungs, but the medic was soon needed to tend to one of the wounded soldiers, and Colley continued the procedure himself. "My heart was hammering so hard," he says, "trying to circulate what little fluid was left in my system, and that's really one of my last clear memories, squeezing on that thing to help myself breathe, and these incredible chest pains that came with it."

For the first time, he noticed the injury to his left arm. He couldn't get his left hand to do what he wanted; the damn thing just wouldn't work. The bones were essentially gone from the center of his hand, and in keeping up the rhythmic squeezing of the air bag he saw what he was dealing with. Doctors later told him that if the hand had been the extent of his injuries, they probably would have tried to save the arm and left Colley with a thumb and little finger. As it was, his injuries were so massive, his blood loss so acute, his condition so weak, they determined to save his life instead.

Even at the mobile hospital, he could feel that death was imminent. Anyway, it was close, and, as a young man of faith, Colley remembers being unafraid. He caught his reflection in those operating room lights, and his reflection's reflection, and it was like he was looking down on himself from above. "I was pressing against that little veil," he says, "thin as a bubble, separates life and death, and I knew at that moment that if I died, I would be in the presence of almighty God, and I haven't wavered from that thought. It's incredible, what I don't remember from that day, but it's also incredible what I do remember. I remember an entire surgical team, scrubbed, wearing that green garb, coming over to where I was, and one of the doctors asking what my blood pressure was. One of the nurses said she couldn't find a pulse, she couldn't get a reading, and I was back to thinking this wasn't good, but then they wheeled me in to the operating room, and it was air conditioned, and I went from thinking the worst to thinking, hey, this isn't so bad after all."

Doctors were fearful of administering a general anesthetic to perform the amputations to Colley's legs and arm, so they summoned one of the men from Colley's company to talk to him through the hours-long procedure. Colley's doctors wanted to keep him alert during the surgery because there was a good chance that if he drifted off into sleep or unconsciousness, they might never get him back. And so, the two men talked. Or, Colley talked and the other man listened. He talked about his home, and his family, and his young bride. He talked about the war. He talked about his career—how it might have been, anyway, before the blast in that open field. At one point, the soldier charged with keeping him company looked down at Colley's wounds and nearly fainted; nurses had to revive him with ammonia so that he could keep going. For years afterward, the soldier told people it was the most difficult thing he ever had to do, keeping that conversation going, trying not to focus on the gory surgery taking place just out of reach.

Of course, Colley lost more than his legs and his arm on that operating room table. He also lost the career he'd spent a lifetime imagining, and, in some ways, that loss was the toughest to take. He'd seen himself in one way, as one thing, for as long as he could remember, and in the space of a few hours, that image had been shattered. He used the next long weeks to recalibrate that image he carried of himself, to set his sights on a new slate of goals.

"I had to get on with it," he says. "Plain and simple. And do you know what? I've never had a nightmare, not one about Vietnam anyway. I've never had flashbacks. Post traumatic stress disorder? I have absolutely no ability to personally identify with it because I don't have it, and I don't even know how to describe it as it relates to my life. I wish I could say it was some kind of willpower that saw me through, but it wasn't that either. It was just, getting on with it, you know. I don't want to minimize how much family support played in all of this, but even before I was reunited with my family, this was how it was. I didn't worry about my wife leaving me because I got injured, that wasn't her nature. She'd written me several times saying that amputees were her favorite patients because they always got better and they learned how to be happy, and I thought, well, by golly, I'll go her one better on that deal. So it just enabled me to get on with my life, turn that page, and not dwell on the negative. I absolutely refused to allow what happened to me that afternoon of July 21st to be the lens through which everything in my life would be viewed. I was going to be in charge of my happiness, my contentment, my sense of self-worth, and my success. I would hold on to those things."

He made two promises to himself as he waited to be transitioned out of Vietnam to a hospital in Japan. He would learn to fly a plane (something he had started to do before enlisting), and he would relearn to water-ski (another pursuit from his pre-injury days). Whatever it took, he would get it done, and he drew extra measures of strength and purpose from the commitments alone.

A month or so later, Colley arrived at Fort Sam Houston in San Antonio, Texas, where twenty-four members of his family had flown to welcome him home. They came to tease, cajole, harass, and otherwise distract him from his grueling rehabilitation, but, at the same time, they were there to offer support. And despite the acceptance and unconditional love of his family, Colley realized he was no longer the same person. He knew this on a fundamental level, but it took seeing himself in the eyes of his family for his outlook to come fully into focus. Obviously, he was no longer six feet tall, one hundred ninety pounds: he was three feet seven and confined to a wheelchair. What wasn't so obvious, and what took a little while to realize, was that his happiness could not in any way be based on what he used to be able to do or weighed against what he could still manage.

"I don't know how I arrived at that," he says, "but early on, it became apparent to me that I better deal with the new guy because the old guy, he's gone. And there are some significant advantages to the person I am today. I used to be somewhat reserved. If I came into a room full of people, I'd kind of migrate up the wall. If you came up and spoke to me, I'd carry on a conversation, but the burden would basically be on you. And that was okay, people could accept that. But if I pulled the same deal in a wheelchair, people would take it the wrong way. They'd look at me as someone who was unhappy or an object to be pitied. And that just pissed me off. Pissed me off so bad that I changed. I became the aggressor. When somebody would catch my eye with that sad, pitying look, I'd go, 'I'm Chad Colley. I don't believe I've met you.' That's the kind of person I became."

Colley wasn't all that taken with the prosthetic technology of the day, but he was fitted for a pair of legs and an arm with a hook where his hand used to be. (There was also a crude, flesh-colored "hand" issued with his prosthetic package, but the thing was so awkward he doesn't think he wore it but a few times.) Even with the prosthetic legs, he needed to use crutches, so he couldn't really see the point of them, but, in the beginning, he wore them to make other people comfortable. The injury to his left leg was so extensive—the femur needed to be removed from the hip socket—that a prosthetic leg was virtually impractical, and the right side wasn't much better, so he soon found that he was better off without the devices. He still keeps a pair of legs, but he hasn't worn them in years, preferring to move about on his own steam. He's gotten to where he can haul himself up and down stairs, in and out of cars, and up and out of bed like it's nothing much at all.

He settled with Betty Ann in Fort Smith, Arkansas, home to both sides of his family, and embarked on a career in real estate sales. It was an unlikely career choice for a man confined to a wheelchair, having to show houses that were rarely wheelchair accessible, with second stories and attics that would have made a lesser man crumble, but Colley determined to make the most of it. "I'll tell you one thing," he says, "when someone came to my office, they would never forget me. They might not remember my name, but they'd remember how I hopped up the three steps to go into the front of the house, hauling my chair behind me."

He must have done something right because he went on to become sales manager for the largest home builder in western Arkansas, was the loan manager of a federal savings and loan association, and was the chief executive officer of a mobile home and land development company near his Forth Smith home.

Colley kept the first of his two promises to himself in no time flat. He got his pilot's license the year he came home to Arkansas, and he bought his first plane a short while after that. But a couple years and a couple kids later, he found he had too much family and too little time to justify the expense of owning his own small plane, so he sold it. And the water-skiing? Well, that took a little bit longer, and he never quite got the hang of it. After designing his own skiing apparatus, he realized that the amount of torque required to pull his body on plane was just too great for his stumps to handle. The only way he could manage it was to recruit friends to help lift him out of the water, and he didn't much like having to rely on others for something that had once been routine, so he redoubled his efforts on the flying front. He found some more time to spend on it and found the money to buy a bigger plane to accommodate his growing family.

But Colley he didn't give up on his skiing plans completely. He decided that maybe he'd hit on the wrong elements and vowed to try snow-skiing instead. He corralled Betty Ann to help him design a homemade contraption that would get him down the mountain in style and in one piece. He got some plaster cast material and an old pair of Levis, and he and Betty Ann managed to fashion a "female" or exterior mold of a lower body. Then they pulled out the clothing, filled the mold with Plaster of Paris, and took the positive mold to a boat

Chad Colley and his wife, Betty Ann

yard where they had it laminated in fiberglass. Colley had no idea if the thing would even work, but he was determined to give it a try. He had it mounted to a ski and shipped to Breckenridge, Colorado.

"By the end of that first day, I had that thing working pretty good," he boasts, "considering it was the first time I'd ever been on anything like that. I had these outrigger poles, which were sort of like crutches with an articulated ski tab, which I used for balance, but nobody had ever seen anything like the contraption we'd designed. And I skied by a group of guys, one of them had a cowboy hat on, so I knew he was from Texas, and we got to talking at the bottom. He told me I was really tearing it up with this thing, and asked how long I'd been skiing on it. I said, 'Oh, about four hours.' He said, 'No, no, I'm not talking about today. I'm talking about your whole life.' I said, 'About four hours.' And this guy just kind of mumbled to himself and walked off."

Soon, Colley was skiing sixty to seventy days per season and tearing it up big time, racing at the very highest levels against comparably able-bodied competition. On the international racing circuit, he says, you run into all kinds of standards as to what constitutes a qualifying disability. On the U.S. team, for example, the more disabled you were, the more opportunities you were given to succeed, but, in competition, Colley found himself skiing against guys who could walk up the mountain and carry their own ski gear. "It always irritated me," he says, "to see a double amputee on the left, and a paraplegic on the right, and in the middle, there'd be some European skier with no limbs missing, some guy able to stand and jump and turn like anybody else."

It hardly seemed sporting, but Colley made certain to beat those guys, too.

In Albertville, France, a hard-charging Colley took first place in two downhill events in the weeks following the 1992 Winter Olympic games, although he wiped out in the slalom, which was usually his strongest event. He skied for the U.S. Ski Team all over the world, winning more often than not, and as he fairly flew down the mountainside, he would think back to the promise he made to himself in his hospital bed in Vietnam. He'd been absolutely convinced that he

Chad Colley

would ski and he would fly, and here he was, doing a world-class job of both at pretty much the same time, although not in quite the same way he'd imagined.

Colley put his real estate career on pause in the middle 1980s to serve as the national commander for Disabled American Veterans. He moved his family to Washington, D.C. for a year. He began giving speeches around the country, testifying before Congress, and standing as a kind of national spokesperson for disabled veterans. The windfall to that experience, he says, was that it got him out and thinking beyond the disabled veteran community. "So much of what we do for disabled veterans has overlapped with the disabled community," he says. "And that's just a real plus. Any victory for veterans that benefits the general population, that's a double-winner. Let's do all we can."

It was that no-limits attitude, coupled with his accelerating accomplishments on the U.S. Ski Team, that called Colley to the attention of the Reagan White House, which honored him as the Handicapped American of the Year in 1986.

Lately, in retirement, Colley's been living a life of semi-leisure, dividing his time between his home in Fort Smith, Arkansas, and his apartment in New Smyrna Beach, Florida, which overlooks the Atlantic Ocean. He and Betty Ann fly back and forth between the two in their own plane, and they manage to squeeze in time for skiing and traveling between visits with their grandchildren. He also chairs the DAV's Committee for the National Disabled Veterans Winter Sports Clinic, which is jointly sponsored by the U.S. Department of Veterans Affairs and the DAV—one of the most extraordinary rehabilitation programs ever organized for the nation's most profoundly handicapped veterans.

His life, he says, is filled to overflowing

Does he ever look back and consider what he's missed, in terms of a military career? "Sure," he admits. "I have my moments. I look at some of my friends who've retired as full colonels or generals and think, that could have been me. But then I look at the other stuff. Not a single one of them has been to dinner at the White House. Not a single one of them has met the pope or Bob Hope or any of the great dignitaries I've been fortunate enough to interact with over the years. So you have to keep things in perspective. Playing all those what-if games takes too much energy, so I just don't go there.

"And besides, nobody's been blessed with the kind of family that I have, especially with the kind of wife that Betty Ann has been. My goodness, everything that people see about me, acknowledge about me, admire about me, they've got to understand that behind that has been a wife who has enabled me to do everything that I have done. Fetching, toting, carrying. Stooping, bending, running, loading. Or, she's been there providing support in that I knew that she loved me enough and cared for what I was about and what I was doing that I didn't have to worry about her finding another interest in her life that would supplant me or interfere with our relationship. People see me standing in the limelight, and Betty Ann's kind of in the shadow off to the side, and that's not how it should be. It's a pretty narrow cone, but she should be right in there with me."

And she is.

THE WAR AT HOME

Richard M. Romley
U.S. Marine Corps, Vietnam War

R ick Romley firmly believes he is richer for his experiences in Vietnam. He is the sort of man whose firm
beliefs fairly define him, and on this one point, he's stead-
fast. He nearly died in a minefield outside of DaNang
near Marble Mountain in a booby-trap explosion that
ultimately cost him both of his legs, but he's convinced he
came back a better person as a result of his injuries.

"I lost so much physically," he says, from his spa-
cious office in the county court building in downtown
Phoenix, where he presides as the Maricopa County
Attorney, "but I gained so much internally. Really, it
made me a better person."

Now, Romley has a reputation as a tough prosecutor and an innovative leader on criminal justice and
community-enrichment issues. It appears that the good
people of Arizona have benefitted as well. Since 1989,
he's headed one of the largest prosecuting attorney's
offices in the country, which serves the fourth most
populated county in the country, and he has done so
with the kind of distinction and effectiveness that people can't help but notice, in Arizona and across the

country. He's testified before Congress and dozens of national organizations on issues such as violent crime, terrorism, drug trafficking, and public corruption. He's been asked by Arizona's Republican Party leaders to consider a run for attorney general (he's not interested), by the Bush Administration to apply for the post of National Drug Czar (he did, but was passed over in favor of John Walters), and to make a gubernatorial run in 2006 (he's thinking about it).

He's endeavored to make a difference in Maricopa County, Arizona, where he grew up. If the awards and plaques and citations decorating his office are any measure of his impact, it would appear that he's done just that. Beneath his varied and mounting accomplishments, Romley credits his harrowing ordeal and grueling recovery with instilling in him the determination and focus that have shaped him as a father, inspired him in business, and informed his career in public service. "I can't see the one without the other," he says. "It's all connected."

Sit across a desk from Rick Romley, with his poised and professional demeanor and his shock of salt-and-pepper hair that looks as if it belongs to a black-and-white matinee idol, and those points of connection become clear. He doesn't shrink from talking about his experiences in Vietnam, but he doesn't advertise them either; they're a part of him, but they don't define him. It's Romley's organized, meticulous, hard-charging personality that comes through most of all. He's got a winning smile that lights up his office and a fit and tan appearance that suggests a life lived in the outdoors instead of in the county courthouse. But looks, as ever,

can be deceiving. Spend a little time with this passion-
ate public servant and the bigger picture emerges: here's
a man who's come through the worst of battle none the
worse for the wear and tear. He may no longer stand on
his own two feet, but he stands tall just the same, and
he means to stand for what's right and good.

It's fitting that a man like Rick Romley makes his life
in and around the Phoenix area—a place the locals
embrace as "the valley of the sun." He belongs here, he
says, and the rugged splendor of the region offers a fine
backdrop to his powerfully sunny disposition. Indeed,
even Romley's call to service had its roots in the valley. He
signed on to the U.S. Marine Corps alongside his best
childhood friend, David Schaffer, with the plan that they
could serve together and worry about college and careers
later. Romley recalls that he was looking for some direction in his life at that time, and he thought the military
experience might help him to find it for himself. His parents were divorced. He'd lived with his father for a stretch,
but wound up living with an aunt. He'd started college,
but his head wasn't in it. He wasn't focused. "Even at that
young age," he says, "I could tell that I needed some structure, some time under my belt. Vietnam was a war in a
distant land. I thought I could do some good, and that
some good would come back to me. I was really a roman-
ticist. I mean, I really was. I read a lot of good guy versus
bad guy comic books as a kid, and I thought of myself as
the kind of guy who could do a little good in this kind of
situation. Not to diminish it or anything, but I would be
the good guy, and fight the good fight. This was April,
1968, and the protesting of the war had just begun around

David Schaffer is on the left, and Romley is on the right

the country, but in the valley, it hadn't really broken out just yet. In the valley, that wasn't really an issue. Our country was at war, and that's what registered."

Romley and Schaffer left for Camp Pendleton on the same bus and returned to Phoenix together after boot camp, where Schaffer stood as best man at Romley's wedding to his high school sweetheart. It was, to hear Romley tell it, a classic "boot camp" wedding. "What can I say?" he asks. "Nobody can tell you anything at that age. We'd dated for a number of years. I don't know that we would have been headed for marriage if it wasn't for the war, but absence makes the heart grow fonder, and boot camp definitely made my heart grow fonder, so we just decided to do it. My orders had come through, and I wanted to have a girl to come home to. It would mean a lot in the field. You know, letters from home are like gold to any soldier."

For Romley and Schaffer, the plan to serve together was pie-in-the-sky. Romley was assigned to Alpha Company, 1st Battalion, 1st Marine Division; Schaffer was assigned to the 3rd Marine Division. The two friends set off linked only in spirit. Romley determined to make the best of his tour, which right away included a harsh adjustment to his new environment. "Right away, I was sent out into the bush, where our command post was," he says. "It was the first night, and I was given guard duty. I was new in country, green as could be, still feeling pretty cocky and invulnerable. And they had this bug juice set out, supposed to keep the mosquitoes away, but they seemed to like it more than anything else. Isn't that always the way? In the morning, when the next guy came to relive me, my face had been eaten by hundreds of mosquitoes. It was unbelievable, what I looked like, but you learn to deal with it, you learn to adjust. In any war, there's always that period of adjustment, like in Iraq with those dust storms. You find a way to adjust. In my case, I never used that bug juice again, and the mosquitoes stopped bothering me."

Romley never got used to some aspects of life in Vietnam: the sweeps that moved from calm to hellfire in the space of a breath, the nightly patrols that seemed to always claim the life of another Marine, the friends who died in each other's arms. If it wasn't one thing, it was another, and the only steadying constants were the mud and the rain and the uncertainty.

Romley and Schaffer didn't write to each other, but Romley's wife was friendly with Schaffer's girlfriend, so the two friends kept tabs through their letters from home. For Romley, there was nothing much to report beyond the ruthless truths of life in a jungle battlefield, until April 7, 1969, about eight and a half months into his tour.

Romley had been made a squad leader, and he was south of DaNang near Marble Mountain with his reinforced squad out on a sweep. There had been some heavy rocketing into DaNang, and Romley was part of a team assigned to determine the source of the rocketing. "It really wasn't supposed to be anything," he says. "We were proceeding cautiously, looking for anything unusual. Looking for bunkers. There was another squad moving alongside of ours, and we were about two-thirds of our way through the sweep, and we came upon this area that was just heavily booby-trapped, and you never knew why an area was heavily booby-trapped. You just knew it when you saw it. Could be it was just an easy geographical location for booby-trapping. Could be there was something they were trying to protect. You just didn't know. All you knew was that you needed to get out of there."

Romley started moving his men out of the mined area, going by the book, but his precautions weren't enough. There was nothing he could have done, that deep into it, and six of his men went down, including his machine gunner. When Romley reached one marine to offer aid and realized that the man had been killed, Romley lifted the man's machine gun and began to carry it out of the field to reassign it to another of his men. It was while he was carrying the machine gun that he stepped where he shouldn't have stepped. "You think back on things," he says, "the things you'd do differently, the decisions you'd like to take back, and I suppose I'd lost focus for a bit. I was carrying that machine gun over my shoulder and grieving for the men we'd just lost and worrying about moving out of that area, and that's when it happened."

Romley tripped a land mine that sent him soaring and tumbling and reeling. There was a whistling noise and then a terrible explosion. He can still recall the pain from the blast, and the noise, and the all-over rush of emotion and worry and second-guessing that came with it. He can still feel the thud his body made against the hard earth. He broke more bones than he knew he had. Two arteries were severed. He was choking on the thick carbonate particles left behind by the explosion. He was gasping for air and trying to get his bearings. The right side of his body was torn up beyond recognition, but he couldn't see extent of the damage. His glasses were blown to the side, so, beyond the pain, he didn't know the extent of his injuries. He thinks now that if he had gotten a good look at how his body had been mangled, he might have slipped into shock. As it was, he had trouble assessing his own situation and holding on. He never lost consciousness, but at the same time, he wasn't clear on anything. The only exchange he can recall from that field was related to him later: a corpsman raced to his side to administer assistance, and the first thing Romley asked after was the family jewels. The corpsman told him he was okay in that area, but he couldn't conceal how far from okay Romley was in almost every other regard. Morphine couldn't chase the pain—not completely. "It helped, some," Romley says, "but boy, when you hurt, you hurt."

Doctors at the Clark Air Force base in the Philippines amputated one leg immediately and worked valiantly to save the other, but Romley's foot and lower leg had been partially blown off. Gangrene developed, and, ultimately, there was no saving it. He was in such furious, unyielding pain that he doesn't recall much of those first few days after the explosion, but he guesses the daily change of dressings will always stay with him. "They couldn't cast the legs to keep them immobile," he says, "because they had to get to them every day, soak down the dressings with a saline solution, where the blood would dry. My whole body was an open wound. Broken bones and open wounds and raw nerves. I was hit everywhere. They'd have to give me a shot before they changed my dressings, it was so painful."

There was no shot for the sickening reality of what Romley was facing, and, as he considered his prospects, his spirits tanked.

The routine, in 1969, was that the military would fly immediate family members to a soldier's hospital bedside if the wounded soldier was not expected to live, even if that bedside was half a world away. Romley fit the bill, and his wife and father made the long trip to Clark Air Force base to be by his side; twenty other families were flown to the Philippines for the same "deathbed" reunion. Romley doesn't remember much beyond the fact of the visit and the fact that every one of those twenty other wounded soldiers eventually died, to a man. "I was the only one who survived," he says, "that's how close I came to dying. None of us were expected to live, but for some reason, I lived."

For a time, doctors were unable to get Romley stable enough to transfer him back to the States, and, in the balance, he started feeling sorry for himself. His spirits tanked even further. He didn't have much fight in him after that minefield, and what little fight there had been was fading fast. He didn't see the point. He didn't know what kind of life awaited him back home, if he even made it back home. He hated the idea of having to rely on others, couldn't see going through life with his hand out, thought how much easier things would have been if he'd died in that minefield. His wife and father had come and gone, and he was left by himself, battling a mess of uncertainty and pain and confusion.

He found a turning point a couple weeks into his stay in the Philippines. Or, he should say, it found him. A young soldier came in, banged up in pretty much the same ways. The poor kid was in agony, Romley recalls. Crying. Wailing. Saying that he couldn't take the pain, that he wanted to die. Romley looked on and saw something of himself, and, in the recognition, he felt himself grow strong. He could never explain it, but there it was. First chance he got, he had himself put near the young soldier. "Hey, look," he said. "I was that way. You've got to fight it. It gets better."

He'd been there all of a couple weeks, and things hadn't gotten any better, not really, and yet here he was, offering words of wisdom and encouragement. *Hey, I was that way.* In reaching out, he felt a purpose reaching back, a reason to keep fighting and moving forward. His spirits lifted. It didn't happen all at once like it does in the movies, but it happened. If he truly believed things would be better, he determined, then he would have to wait out the dark patches. He'd have to practice what he found himself inexplicably preaching.

"I must have had twenty surgeries over there before they stabilized me," he says. "I was miserable. I don't think I was in any kind of shape to be handing out advice, but that was a real lifesaver for me. Got me to see my own situation from a different perspective."

Soon after, Romley did a complete about-face. He went from fighting to survive to fighting to thrive. His wounds weren't healing on any kind of hoped-for timetable, but in his head he was making plans for his future, figuring his next moves. When he was finally transferred to Balboa Naval Hospital in San Diego, where he lost the fight to keep his other leg, he overheard his sister out in the hallway, wondering, "My God, what is he going to do with himself for the rest of his life?" She didn't mean anything by it, he knew, but it rankled him just the same. And it made him stronger. He got a game plan together that would help him lead what he called an "undisabled" life. He wanted to do as much as he possibly could, as quickly as he possibly could, as well as he possibly could. Nothing would be out of reach. He went back to school. He learned how to maneuver on his prosthetic legs. He and his wife talked about starting a family.

The trouble was, Romley's wife was slower to make the adjustment to Romley's new reality, and, one year after the explosion, he found himself back home in Arizona with two young sons coming and a marriage breathing its last. He wound up with custody of the kids, and he flashed back to the time he spent in his father's household after his parents' divorce. It was the same, but different. He was struggling to relearn to walk himself and, at the same time, chasing his boys through their first paces. He discovered that upper body strength was key—in lifting a toddler from the floor or picking himself up after a fall—and that what at first seems like everything in the end might appear as nothing much at all.

"It was a challenge," he says in his self-deprecating way, "but we got through it okay."

Somehow, Romley managed to find time to earn his business management degree at Arizona State University, graduating with honors in 1974, after which he built and operated a successful retail business. For the first time, he was headed down a purposeful path. On any given day, he couldn't tell you which was more difficult, being a single parent or a bilateral, above-the-knee amputee, but in the confluence of hardships, he prospered. The direction and focus he'd lacked during his first college try he now had in abundance, and as his business took off, his dreams took off with it. It was one thing to make a living, he found himself thinking, and quite another to make a difference. He started to think about law school—he'd come from a long line of lawyers—with an eye toward public service of some kind, and he sold his business and re-upped at Arizona State, this time headed for his Juris Doctorate.

"By the time I was in law school, I was moving about pretty good," he says. "I was used to my prosthetics and walking with a cane, and the kids were more independent each year. The morning was my time. I'd get up early, work out, study, do whatever I had to do before the day got away from me. Nights were for the kids."

Romley's days were no less busy once he got out of law school and signed on as an assistant district attorney. He'd never seriously considered a move into private practice or corporate law, and he felt it was his civic and patriotic duty to give something back to his community. Where he came up with this equation, he's got no idea. He'd already given so much, but he didn't see things that way. He didn't see that answering the call to fight a war overseas excused him from an obligation to set things right at home. He didn't see how a cushy, private sector job would improve the quality of life in Maricopa County for his children, for his friends and neighbors, for the folks he'd never even meet. And so he went to work in the County Attorney's office and set about making that difference.

He also met and married his current wife, Carol, and gained a stepson. Once again, he turned his sights to bigger and better things. In 1988, he ran for county attorney. He was thirty-eight years old and says now he had no business reaching for so much so soon, but he reached just the same. And the voters responded, electing Romley to one of the biggest law enforcement jobs in the country. He had no political experience, but he figured politics didn't matter; you never know if the bad guys are Republicans or Democrats when you're trying to keep them off the streets.

As county attorney, Romley has been a relentless prosecutor and a courageous agent of change. He successfully prosecuted the largest public corruption case in Arizona's history. His office's anti-drug diversion effort, the Maricopa County Demand Reduction Program, became a model for communities nationwide and was adopted by the president's Drug Advisory Committee. He helped to rewrite Arizona's Criminal Code, leading a "truth in sentencing" movement that now requires convicted criminals to serve their full sentences. Wherever possible, he's combined tough law enforcement with aggressive prevention efforts, and the results have been astonishing. Even his Democratic opponents concede that the Phoenix area is much cleaner and safer on Rick Romley's watch, and it's no wonder.

In a position paper entitled "A Nation and its Drugs," which was presented to the Bush Administration when he was being considered for the post of Drug Czar, Romley laid out some of his proposals for safeguarding our youth in the war on drugs. He wrote:

> In our past efforts, America has met with successes and has seen some failures as well. We should learn from this and keep what has worked and not be afraid to discard what has not worked. One thing is certain: our main problem is not from Bogota, Colombia, but from within America. Unless we reduce the demand for drugs in our country and change the

'cultural acceptance' of these drugs, all of our efforts will be inadequate. It is time for our priorities to shift to prevention and treatment. . . .

We should not harbor the false illusion that drugs will be totally erased from our society, but we can do better. We can do better only if there is strong leadership that unites our country behind a rational and compassionate strategy. America deserves nothing less.

He's felt the same way about the good people of Maricopa County—that they deserve nothing less than his best efforts, in and out of the courtroom. Indeed, throughout his four terms as county attorney, Romley has reached beyond the traditional role of prosecutor. "Fifteen years ago, I don't think I really understood what it meant to be successful as a district attorney of a major metropolitan area," he says. "My role is not just to be successful in the courtroom. That's part of it, sure, but we've also got to work to reduce crime, to cut down on drug and alcohol use, particularly among our young people. We've got to work at the front end, on issues of prevention, to make our communities safer.

"We're a city on the rise. Our Diamondbacks beat the Yankees in the World Series. We've got a terrific new stadium, and our office was a part of that. People know me as a prosecutor, but I'm also the civil attorney for the county, and we were out in front on the public-private partnership that had to be created in the building of that stadium. Education issues. Health-care issues. We're across the board."

A run for governor is not out of the question, but Romley is not about to oppose the current governor, Janet Napolitano, a Democrat, if he feels she's doing a good job when the office is up for grabs in 2006. "She's just starting her first term," he says, "but so far she's doing some good things and she has my full support. Do I agree with every position she's taken? No, but I like what I see. It's not about politics for me. I don't like running for office. I've got to have my heart in it if I'm going to be effective, and if there's no compelling reason to run, then I just won't run. I'm not going to do it just to do it."

Like many combat-wounded veterans, Romley notes the anniversary of his injuries in his own private way. He measures the passage of time and pauses to reflect on the course his life has taken in the intervening years. He keeps a box of letters, audio tapes, and official documents from his time in Vietnam, which he means to open and review on his fifty-fifth birthday. He doesn't need to sift through those memories just yet, but he knows the day will come when they will be a part of him once more. He'll hole himself up for a month or so and sort through the mess of memory.

He noted with particular interest the anniversary that left him wounded for longer than he'd been whole. "That was strange," he says, "to think of yourself in your mind's eye as a fully able-bodied individual, and to realize that that hasn't been the case in the longest time."

The most recent anniversary was perhaps the strangest and most troubling of all. On the seventh of April, 2003, Romley's son, Captain David Romley,

USMC, was stationed in Baghdad, when the fighting in Iraq was still hot and heavy. "I was a little superstitious," Romley says. "I came to work, did my job, same as any other day, but I thought about it. All day long I thought about it. I thought, my God, it's April 7th. My day. My son's in combat. It was an uneasy day."

Thankfully, David Romley made it through that day without incident—and through every day since. His father has kept close through e-mails and photos. It's a different war, Rick Romley can't help but notice. A different time. A different generation. Back in his day, it could take weeks for a letter to reach its destination—months, even—but now if you don't get an e-mail for a day or two, you start to worry.

There's another date that stands out on Romley's calendar, as it does with most veterans. Each Memorial Day, he collects flowers from his own yard and places them at the base of one of the black granite slabs at the Arizona Vietnam Veterans Memorial in Phoenix. If he pulls enough flowers, they can just about reach to the ninth name from the bottom: *Schaffer, David Thomas, Lance Corporal, United States Marine Corps.*

Schaffer was killed in a sapper attack near the DMZ in August, 1969, just a few weeks before his tour was due to end. He'd known about Romley's injuries through his letters from home, and from what Romley later heard, he was devastated by the news, but the two friends never communicated directly from the moment they went overseas. In fact, Romley didn't even know the circumstances of Schaffer's death until Romley was honored in 2001 as the outstanding disabled veteran of the year by the Disabled American Veterans. A resulting profile in the DAV magazine yielded an e-mail response from a marine who had been in Schaffer's unit, who kindly filled Romley in on the missing details. "Of course, it couldn't bring him back," he says, "but you want to know what happened."

After Schaffer's death, his parents gave Romley their son's Marine Corps ring, which he had bought when he was in boot camp. Romley kept it and drew strength from it, thinking back on his friend and the decision they made to throw in together as marines. Romley carried that ring until he passed it on to his son, David Thomas Romley, named for his fallen friend. David Romley attended officer candidate school and has made the Marine Corps a career. "It's a good connection," Romley says of his buddy's ring. "A meaningful connection. And it's served us well."

The good people of Maricopa County might say the same of Rick Romley, who's served them well for a good long while, and means to do so for the next while.

CLOSING STATEMENT

Jesse Brown made quite an impression. I only had the honor of meeting him once, at his home in Warrenton, Virginia, and for Jesse it was getting late in the game. He'd been diagnosed with amyotrophic lateral sclerosis, also known as Lou Gehrig's Disease, and he wasn't having a great morning when I showed up. I never got that from Jesse, though. His devoted wife Sylvia greeted me at the door and gently asked if I would mind taking a stroll around town for an hour or two, in the hope that Jesse might be feeling a little stronger after a couple hours rest. Of course, I didn't mind. It was early spring, and there were worse ways to kill some time than to stroll through Old Town Warrenton.

Plus, I'd come all this way to meet a man who was fairly revered by millions of American veterans. I wanted to shake this man's hand, see what all the fuss was about, so I wasn't in any rush to head home.

ALS is a cruel neuromuscular disease that slowly robs its victims of the ability to move, speak, swallow, and breathe without assistance; its degenerative effects can be felt over a period of months or years. Most ALS patients die within three to six years of onset. Some die sooner. All die eventually. There is no known cure and no discernible cause. I knew what to expect, hopping the shuttle down to Washington, D.C., and renting a car for the short drive out to Jesse's home, but, at the same time, I had no idea. Jesse and I had communicated through e-mail, mostly, and through intermediaries, and as I browsed through quaint souvenir stores with shelves devoted mainly to Civil War memorabilia and merchandise, it occurred to me that the two of us had not yet spoken. I thought it strange that I hadn't considered this small detail until just this moment. It had all seemed quite natural to arrange a first meeting through left-behind messages and e-mail, or through interested third parties.

For the longest time, Jesse Brown held out on even his closest friends. He hated the absolute aspects of this disease, the way it left him without even a fighting chance, and so he put off telling people about it for as long as he possibly could. He wasn't being deceitful, and he wasn't in any kind of denial, but he wanted to forestall the finality of every exchange that would follow his disclosure. He didn't want to see how he looked in the eyes of his friends and family until there was no turning away, but when he finally came clean, he was in for a surprise. The folks who knew him best were not prepared to write Jesse off. They continued to come to him for advice. They continued to plan for a shared future. They continued to advance long-term projects with which Jesse had been involved. The ALS offered no fighting chance, but Jesse would fight it just the same. He'd keep living his life in what ways he could.

This much I knew before knocking on his door that spring morning. And I knew a few things more. I knew that Jesse Brown had been U.S. secretary of veterans' affairs—a cabinet-level position bestowed upon him by President Bill Clinton—and that his relentless, proud leadership and advocacy efforts cast him as a kind of hero among American veterans, particularly among his fellow disabled veterans. I knew that under Jesse's stewardship, the VA expanded benefits for veterans who had been prisoners of war or who had been exposed to Agent Orange, radiation, or mustard gas. I knew that he helped to lead an investigation into the possible causes of unexplained illnesses among Persian Gulf War veterans and championed legislation that provided priority health care to those affected. And I knew that on his watch, the VA had expanded services to women veterans, including counseling for sexual trauma suffered in the military and hiring more full-time coordinators for women's care at VA medical centers.

"Anyone who puts his or her life on the line deserves to be treated with the utmost dignity and respect," he once told a newspaper reporter, and the line was more than just a line to Jesse Brown. The words were more than words. They were his marching orders.

I knew something of his service record, too. He'd been wounded as a young marine on patrol near

DaNang in 1965, hit in a hellish firefight that left his right arm partially paralyzed, and he came home to the United States determined not to become another depressing statistic in VA journals. He would make something of himself. He would make a difference.

As it happened, he made that difference helping others in a long, distinguished career with the nonprofit Disabled American Veterans organization, which he joined in 1967 as a national service officer in Chicago. He was named deputy national service director in 1983, and served as executive director of the DAV's Washington headquarters from 1989 until January, 1993. Then he was sworn in as secretary of veterans affairs, the federal government's second largest department, responsible for the care and benefits of nearly 25 million veterans.

All of this was part of Jesse Brown's public record, which is accessible through a couple keystrokes on the Internet, but what failed to come across in my electronic search was the deep and lasting impact he'd made with veterans across the country. The connections he'd forged over the years. The profoundly positive differences he'd been able to make and maintain. No search engine could convey the sheer strength of character that would find me on the other side of Jesse Brown's front door when I returned after a few hours away, the vitality that even a wasting disease like ALS couldn't kill.

Jesse's big brown eyes filled in the blanks of his story.

He was propped up in a reclining chair in the family room of his beautiful home. His speech was painstakingly slow and labored. He couldn't move at all by this point, but I took his hand anyway and shook it in greeting. We visited for about an hour, focused mainly on a book Jesse wanted to write. He didn't want to write about himself, he said, but he wanted to shine a light on some of the wonderfully courageous individuals he'd befriended over the years. He felt that in sharing their stories, the American people would be better able to understand what it means to pick up the pieces of a shattered life after a disabling injury, what it takes to dedicate yourself to a lifetime of service only to have that service interrupted and that lifetime redefined.

Jesse had reached out to me through his good friend Lois Pope. The two of them thought that a book about disabled American veterans would help to call positive attention to their effort to build a national memorial to disabled veterans in Washington, D.C., and as I sat there and listened to Jesse struggle to communicate his passion for each project, I found myself looking deeply into his eyes. They were alive, with moment and purpose and possibility. The disease couldn't touch those eyes. They did his smiling. They told me what his words could not. They told me what that fuss was all about.

What came out of that meeting was this: I would work off a list of prospective subjects of disabled American veterans that Jesse had compiled and begin the attendant research. Jesse would do what he could from his computer, with his wife Sylvia's help, to add to that list and to supplement that research. He'd also dispatch his good friend and fellow marine Charlie Thompson, whose profile appears in these pages and who lived nearby, to act as go-between and to introduce me to individuals we wanted to consider for interviews. We'd share our findings electronically, again with Sylvia's help, and whittle our unmanageable list of worthy candidates to a manageable few dozen. Ultimately, I would travel the country to meet with the dozen or so veterans we wanted to profile, and to interview them on Jesse's behalf.

For a while, the project moved forward according to plan. Jesse was a dedicated and enthusiastic writing partner. I'd send him sample passages to consider, and he'd quickly return them with his insightful commentary. Or, he'd send material to me that he wanted to include. Things went on in this way for several months, and Jesse was determined to beat the disease to its deadline, but, eventually, the back-and-forth in our electronic working relationship became difficult. There was more and more time between query and response. Jesse's enthusiasm for the book had not been stilled, Sylvia assured me, but his ability to keep up with his enthusiasm was not what it was.

Soon—too soon—the disease won out.

Jesse died on August 15, 2002, and with his passing a light went out on his hoped-for book project. I set our efforts aside and counted myself lucky for having known such a remarkable man, even in such a fleeting, once-removed way. We'd given Jesse's book our best shot, but, in the end, we couldn't research and write the thing quickly enough for the ALS. There would still be a memorial in Washington, but it would have to find its way to groundbreaking and completion without the jump-start Jesse hoped to offer with his book.

And then a curious and marvelous thing happened. Lois Pope telephoned one afternoon and asked if I would take up the book project once more, in Jesse's memory. Sylvia Brown very much wanted us to see the book through to publication, she said, and the feeling among the leaders at the Disabled Veterans Life Memorial Foundation, which was spearheading the memorial effort, was that Jesse's collection of inspiring, inspiriting profiles would go a powerfully long way toward seeing that effort realized. I contacted Charlie Thompson to see if he would resume his role as liaison between my civilian self and Jesse's military community, and he was all too happy to sign back on. Indeed, he was thrilled. "I've only met a few men in my life who I would again follow into combat," he told me, in agreeing to pick up where we'd left off. "J.B. was one of them."

I consulted Charlie again when I was thinking about this coda to the book. I was fishing for some appropriate way to tip my pen to Jesse—for setting this project in motion, and for letting me pinch from his legacy to see it through—and Charlie suggested there was only one fitting send-off, which he'd like to make himself, from marine to marine: "*Semper Fi*, my good friend." Of course, as a civilian, it wouldn't do for me to bend such a time-honored tradition of the corps for this right here, but, as a journalist, I can certainly quote from Charlie directly.

And so, in closing, I offer this: what Charlie said.

Daniel Paisner
August 15, 2003

ABOUT THE AUTHORS

Jesse Brown
U.S. Marines, Vietnam War

Jesse Brown was a young marine on patrol near DaNang in 1965, when a vicious firefight left his right arm partially paralyzed. After he was injured, he redirected his thinking to focus on what he could still accomplish, instead of what he could no longer manage. Facing a lifetime of disability, he heard the call to serve his fellow disabled veterans, and he joined the professional staff of the nonprofit organization, Disabled American Veterans (DAV) in 1967.

For the next thirty-three years, his service and dedication earned him the respect and admiration of those at the highest levels of government, culminating in his appointment as U.S. secretary of veterans' affairs under President Bill Clinton. Under Secretary Brown's leadership, the VA expanded benefits for veterans who were prisoners of war or were exposed to Agent Orange, radiation, or mustard gas. Secretary Brown also directed the development of new homeless veterans programs at VA medical centers nationwide. After leaving the VA in 1997, he served with distinction as the executive director of the Disabled Veterans' Life Memorial Foundation, where he worked to create the first national memorial to honor disabled American veterans from all wars. He died in August, 2003, after a long battle with amyotrophic lateral sclerosis (ALS).

Daniel Paisner is one of the busiest collaborators in publishing. He has helped to write dozens of best-selling and headline-making books with prominent entertainers, athletes, business leaders, and politicians. He has worked with Whoopi Goldberg, Anthony Quinn, Geraldo Rivera, New York governor George Pataki, former New York mayor Ed Koch, bilateral amputee mountaineer Ed Hommer, and FDNY battalion commander Richard Picciotto, whose account of his epic tour of duty on September 11, 2001, *Last Man Down,* became an international bestseller. His second novel, *Mourning Wood,* will be published by Volt Press in January 2004.